THE SAVANTASSE OF MONTPARNASSE

OVERLEAF: *The Savantasse of Montparnasse*

ALLEN MANDELBAUM

The Savantasse
of Montparnasse

WITH TEN DRAWINGS FROM
«THE SAVANTASSE SCROLLS».
BY MARIALUISA DE ROMANS

A CONVIVIO BOOK

SHEEP MEADOW PRESS · NEW YORK

SHEEP MEADOW PRESS
Riverdale-on-Hudson, New York

Distributed by Persea Books

ISBN 0-935296-70-0
ISBN 0-935926-71-9 (paper)

PRINTED IN ITALY

OTHER BOOKS BY ALLEN MANDELBAUM

POETRY

Journeyman, 1967

Leaves of Absence, 1976

Chelmaxioms: The Maxims, Axioms, Maxioms of Chelm, 1978

A Lied of Letterpress, 1980

VERSE TRANSLATIONS/EDITIONS

Life of a Man by Giuseppe Ungaretti, 1958

Selected Writings of Salvatore Quasimodo, 1960

The Aeneid of Virgil, 1972 (National Book Award, 1973), 1981

Selected Poems of Giuseppe Ungaretti, 1975

Inferno of Dante, 1980

Purgatorio of Dante, 1982

Paradiso of Dante, 1984

Ovid in Sicily, 1986

The Odyssey of Homer (forthcoming)

CONTENTS

THE SAVANTASSE OF MONTPARNASSE

FIRSTLIGHT

            descends the serpent Seine.
It fords two shuttered panes and then
my dim divan in this Hôtel
du Mi-Chemin near Rue Grenelle.

La nuit s'en va, et ses chandelles . . .
Some ninety lines away, a bell-
tower wakes. It tolls. My tale's
impatient Incipit impels.

Firstlight. Yet I, before I cross
the gate that guards recountings, must
meet once again that shade whom I
first met by candlelight, in times

when tempests on pre-Alpine nights
(the place, a Piedmontese lakeside)
had cut the current, and my eyes
would conjure one who could contrive—

within the hemisphere of light
a candle cast across the half-
moon table where I sat beside
his *Metamorphoses*—to meet

both weightless things and things of weight,
fantasques mismatched, the nomad shapes
of man and animal and plant
and gods, with unabated chant.

And thought of that has brought to mind
(still other time, still other site)
our meeting in the Apennines,
where—on Sulmona's central square—

his bronze and brooding effigy
had overlooked our colloquy
beneath a sun so lucid we
were driven into clarity.

Thus, it would seem, as some aver,
that tutelary shades observe
no calendar: they know that life
is lived in longing, and arrive

whenever living hands implore
by candle-, star-, dawn-, noon-light, or
within the tenebrae. Therefore,
I call upon Sulmona's son,

the guardian of nervous forms'
courbures, détours, délabrements,
décrépissages, résurrections,
in all of time's arrondissements:

Ovidius-The-Garrulous,
The-Copious, The Ever-Swift,
Amir-Of-Metamorphosists,
and Sad-Seigneur-Of-Scrutinists,

The-Exiled-One, I pray, assist
me now as I confront the *songe*,
vapeur, *lueur*, and *fleur* my song
must summon to embody one

who sipped from cracked carafes on Mont
Parnasse. May my long love for your
hexameter (though briefer line
and matter less divine are mine—

my fable less enshrined) incite
a serpentine that can inscribe
the *savantasse*—yet not elide
his waywardness. Ovidius,

as dawn descends the seaward Seine,
entwining origins and ends
of *rue*s that rush and *rue*s that wend,
as bridges, quays, and domes, gargoyles,

belltowers, silent spires, and vowels
and consonants are caught in coils
of one conspiring sun, abet
this book, this confluence—more deft,

more various than any I
can weave, devise, or thieve unless
your calamus contrive as my
confederate. Ovidius,

la nuit s'en va, et ses chandelles . . .
Permit these parts and whole to dwell
at peace with one another: free
my chant from dark discrepancy.

Against the trials of negligence,
digressions, lapses, indolence,
that—many warn—beset the course
of rivers, *rues*, and metamorphs,

against the hell of lone divans
in that Hôtel du Mi-Chemin
where soul of man or woman needs
to reach the doors of reverie

or dream, and finds that these bequeath
no lied—only débris, *dédales*,
walls scrawled with stunted syllables,
dismembered, dim, inscrutable,

be shield and shelterer. Befriend.
Give me the strength to see The-End.
May your fraternal hand extend
across the passage-points of death

and life, to touch this weaver and
this web; and your fraternal breath
sustain, support, be staff and stead
for both The-Reader and The-Read.

PRECAUTIONARY PRELUDE

The *savantasse* of Montparnasse
was—some contend—the only un-
enlightened son descended from
the vowels of the hoarse savant
and his disheveled consonants.
But who had mothered him? And when?
And where: on what distraught divan
or in discreet *pinarium*?
And did he love with long incest
when he remembered Greta Lentz?
But in the shadowed atrium
that fronts the grey Musée de l'Homme
(just where the fountain of Chopin
would chant the *moira* of all men
and women: sorrow and chagrin—
o *moia biéda*—and the hymn
of reconciliation), when
the transient lanterns have been spent,
the plight of the approximate
afflicts impatient Querists: mist
resists the rites of certainty—
the lines of genealogy,
the protocol of family,
the stemmas and the variants,
are victims of the black Vortex-
Of-*Nebel*-Night-*Néant*-And-*Nichts*-
And-Tenebrae-That-Scoff—as if
light were still-born in genesis.

Yet once the act of origin
is past, the long vicissitudes

of exodus and aftermath
provide the unelusive clues
so kin in kind to certitudes
that Night itself cannot refute
their blue verisimilitude:
we know the savantasse—at last—
had crossed the plain of Montparnasse
and, in his crossing, often paused
to rest his worn astragalus
along the languid Rue Lebouis
and other dilatory streets
and, furthermore, are certain he
had witnessed, as he lingered, three
incontrovertible graffiti
etched in one-hundred-seventy-
three unassuming majuscules
upon the unimpatient walls
that overlooked his reveries
(and from the walls, he took them as
precautionary epigraphs,
his burdens for diurnal chants
that found themselves nocturnal when
agrypnia held his tarboosh
too fast when he was hard upon
his *Jacaranda-Liederbuch*
or *Ayres-To-Exorcise-Despair*
From-Carrefours-Where-Paths-Of-Parts-
Are-Gathered-In-A-Great-Gestalt-
And, There-Assembled, Find-The-All-
Is-But-Another, Crueler-Cul-
De-Sac: The-Unendurable),

and these graffiti surely were:

LA CHAIR EST TRISTE, HÉLAS! ET J'AI
LU TOUS LES LIVRES.　　—　　TOUT
LE MALHEUR DES HOMMES VIENT D'UNE
SEULE CHOSE, QUI EST DE NE SAVOIR
PAS DEMEURER EN REPOS DANS UNE
CHAMBRE.　　—　　LE SILENCE ÉTERNEL
DE CES ESPACES INFINIS M'EFFRAIE.

But even such decisive clues
(the majuscules and very *rue*s
that saw the harassed *savantasse,*
with or without his compass, pass)
will soon succumb beneath the ax
of urban resurrection that
may promise birth but hacks to death
the pensive plain of Montparnasse,
converting into dark debris
the walls and halls of Rue Lebouis
and Rue Jules-Guesde and Rue de l'Ouest
as well as Rue Vercingétorix
(of which, when *rue*s return to dust
in the fourteenth arrondissement,
even the patient may omit—
or err in their misplacing it—
the plaintive secondary stress
that falls and calls—like a *rossignol*—
upon the pliant syllable
that is the third among the six
that live in Rue-Ver-*cin*-gé-to-rix),　·

until the streets and epigraphs
and solaces of Montparnasse
are simply flatus vocis for
this prelude, which must stand before
the stanzas of the dispossessed:
that is to say, the space the ear
and heart allot to what is past.

And what has passed has need of more
than flatus vocis to restore
Before to Now—as even those
timorous River-Hearers, souls
who never stir to sail the course
of waters (passive, perilous,
or just equanimous, that rush
or idle toward a confluence
in ever-murmuring synagogue,
The-Congregation-Of-The-Parts,
with their fraternal river gods
or toward the more paternal sea
or, some say, its maternity,
by way of inlet, estuary,
or more insidious entry),
but, sedentary, merely hear
(while at their back a samovar
dispenses teas from Tirich Mir
as they consult the *Gazetteer-
For-Sleepless-Gluteists*) the flow
of labials and laterals
and dentals, nasals, laminals,
and alveolars, palatals,

occlusives, spirants, fricatives,
implosives, flaps, and stops and clicks,
ingressives, liquids, sibilants,
and gutturals in the Garonne,
the Godavari, Swat, Saône,
the Cère, Var, Lot, Ance, Rance, Oust, Lauze,
Baup, Lauch, Auze, Aude, Orb, Save, Gave, Lez,
Aure, Hers, Gard, Touch, Cher, Têt, Arse, Cèze,
Couze, Neste, Nauze, Dropt, Doubs, Dasht, Fecht, Bès,
Tay, Spey, Dee, Tweed, Osse, Orge, North Esk,
the Tunghabadra, Chip Chap, Claise,
the Stour, Styr, Styx, Bouzaize, and Ouche,
Dourdou and Dheune and Restigouche,
the Kuskokwim, the Oknagan,
the Tagus, Tigris, Sambatyón,
the Xanthus, Kishon, Acheron,
the Hudson and the Phlegethon,
the Pend Oreilles, the Petitot,
the Pedernales and the Po,
the Seine, Eunoe, Lethe—know.
Even the dimmest *sédentaire*,
the River-Hearer least aware,
the Syllabite content to share
no more than sounds with streams and streets,
concedes that *rue*s, like rivers, need
more than a naming if their shores
would serve as sojourn for a choir
of souls incongruous as those
encountered by the *savantasse*
on thoroughfares and culs-de-sac
where he considered Alls and Parts—

and may have tracked The-Tousled-Ox—
in metamorphic Montparnasse:

the undemanding FRAU PERFORCE,
who—after her abrupt divorce
from woodways in the far Black Forest—
had hoped to reach the Rue Descartes
(or, lacking that, another path
devoted to an *echt* savant)
within the fifth arrondissement,
but fell on Montparnasse instead
(by way—some say—of a couchette
that overran the Gare de l'Est)
and there, not far from Rue Jules-Guesde,
compiled her unobtrusive *Precepts*;

and then SOUDAINE SOUPLESSE, who dressed
in citron sagathy *sans feinte*
et artifice and always left
no *ens* to be desired when she
addressed herself to tenderness
by lamplight on the Rue de l'Ouest;

and even ENTHYMEME, who found—
by way of winters she had spent,
inclement, on the Rue de Rennes—
that syllogistic streets, of which
the fifth and sixth arrondissements
were far too full, were seldom fit
for shepherding non-sequiturs
across astonished carrefours

and moved to Mont Parnasse therefor;

or ANGÉLIQUE ABRÍ, who—since
she lived along the Cherche-Midi,
as some allege—was often prone
to cycle south to Rue Lebouis
and parley there on Pierre Proudhon
and Claude-Henri de Saint-Simon,
since southern pavements often can
shed light on the utopian
Promenade des Horizons
(or the Hallucinarium
in which the lens of Charles Fourier,
extending his anatomy
of Twelve-Pervasive-Passions we
must feel when, free of grey ennui,
we sack the stores of reverie's
Polygamy, Amphigamy,
Omnigamy, Celadony,
had understood no passion should—
since every passion is a good—
confound, collide with, or confute
another passion and concludes
that love concupiscent as well
as love of family are best
reconciled in tranquil incest);

and MAUD MARAUD, who held her mind
must be the stand on which a bright
mirror stood and therefore wiped
it—diligently—free of dust

and, once she had erased her past,
would scavenge others' antefacts
instead (their unforgotten acts
of sudden sin and pondered wrath,
deceit, abandonment, neglect—
for which she probed her *amadors'*
confessionals with preying words)
until sufficient evidence
had, in her talons, been assembled
to make the most impeccable—
the most detached—*sanyāssin* tremble;

and dour Ecclesiastesists—
but witness HERR SCHWARZSEHER, who
had never thought to find a room
where an expatriate might choose
to overflow with *amertume*
(as he assessed the *vanitas*
of planting trees, expending breath,
aligning tender vines, the sweat
of time that sews and time that rends
tendons and nerves and ligaments,
the stones we cast, the flight from them,
the bile, the lymph, the blood, the phlegm,
hair of the body, hair of the head,
the nails, the skin, the teeth, the seed
we breed, the thread we weave, the drum
that jars the telencephalon,
and Disquisition's-Double-Gong
that sounds with struck and unstruck sounds,
the rice, the kidney beans, the bread,

the time to lose, the time to get,
the conscientiousness, the sloth,
the time to track The-Tousled-Ox,
the season of discrepant flocks,
the veil to screen, the veil to vex,
the plague of faith, the plague of hope,
the unavailing antidotes,
the tatters, the erratic texts,
the purgatives, the poultices,
the Gare du Nord, the Gare de l'Est,
the vigil, the forgetfulness,
on his exhausted abacus)
till Montparnasse provided one;

and ALEXANDER-THE-SLEEPLESS,
whose cilia were always bent
upon The-Indiscernible
within the shadowed atrium
of the Musée de l'Homme until
the Rue de Galimatias
afforded him (together with
his *mens* and other kin and kith
dependent on his indigence)
the refuge of a room well-lit,
with four and finite saffron walls
and seven window-panes—and none
that overlooked oblivion—
so long as he had shuttered them.

To which a few append: No shore
or *rue* that did not offer more

than name alone could shelter forms
as palpable as those Wen Tong
envisioned when his brush had drawn
his Final-Scroll, which often hung
above the devious divan
whereon the *savantasse* collapsed
when each of his Twelve-Passions and
all thoughts on Parts and Alls were spent
and Nothing-Less-Than-Nothingness
might well have been all he had left
of his progenitors' bequest—
last residue of genesis—
were he without that rhomboid scroll
to render The-Discernible,
to thwart The-Unconsolable.

One

THE CRACKED CARAFE

The Cracked Carafe

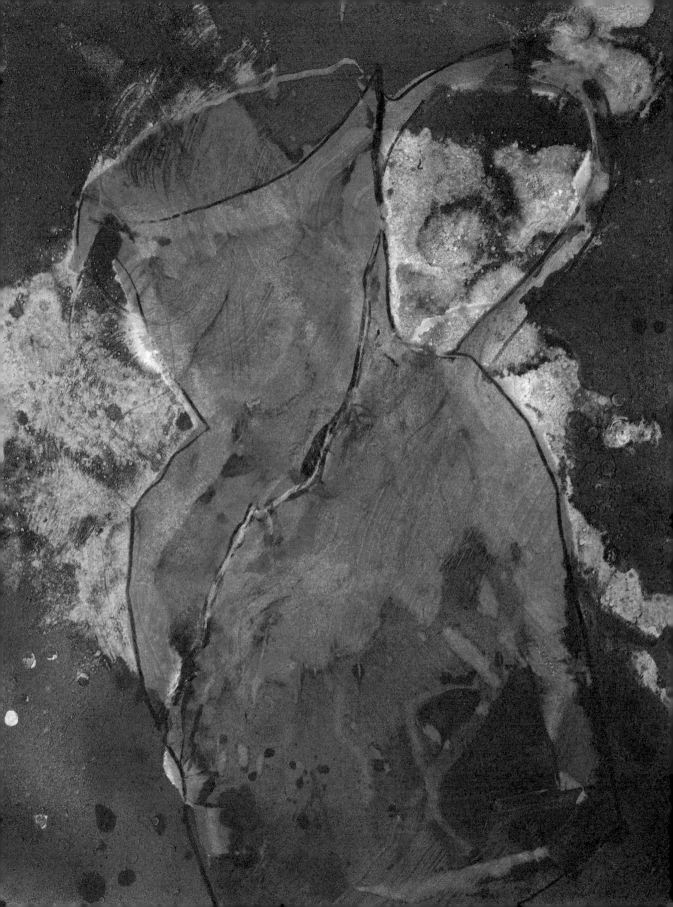

BEFORE THE BRUSH

They say that when he painted shoots he too became bamboo.
Should this be true, and not the inks alone but you
transform, remember, then, Wen Tong, who
weighed each shape he would depict:
forget   the   jacaranda's
hectic; draw a
possumhaw.

THE AYRE OF THE *TRISTE CHAIR*

Some say Signora Enthymeme
(though ten contend it may have been
Soudaine Souplesse or Frau Perforce

or even Maud Maraud) unhorsed
a *savantasse* of Montparnasse—
more lecherous than learned—who

would gallop north as far as Rue
de Rennes whenever rumor ran
(and disconcerted his divan,

his lectern, lantern, dais, and
his paperweight from the Kuskokwim,
savanna-green linoleum,

and prayer rug from Kirsehir
and far too tarnished samovar
and cracked carafe of tafia

and suasive scenes the aging Wen
Tong painted on a scroll as brief
as breath within the woods of grief

or long as ruminations seem
as soon as Honey-Be recedes)
with word that some had seen within

The-Scuffed-Sabots: *Two-Guides-To-Parts-*
Of-Speech-Along-The-Rue-d'Assas,
compiled by Angélique Abrí

(while pedalling to Saint-Sulpice,
despite the slabby winter mists,
from her retreat on the Cherche-Midi),

a savantasse impoverished,
denied, deprived, defined as this:
«A masculine noun, meaning sciolist».

But once, when he had hurried north
in search of tercets that might nurse
his hurt, and burst on Enthymeme,

she only turned (as she reversed
her iridescent earrings, green
odóndonite above her cunning

bayadere of bombazeen)
to hum *Ah! non credea mirarti*
and murmur unassuagingly:

«His books are sad, alas: he has
read all the flesh but read it as
an unconversant Paraphrast

(or sedentary Scrutinist
bewildered by his pale pastis),
a browser, not a lover—one

who comes upon the colophon
before the text has time to ask
the quaere that will crack his

exegesis».

THE AYRE OF ALL

The *savantasse*
of Montparnasse,
in tan tarboosh

and black surtout,
had long confused
the Hindu Kush

with Tirich Mir.
But when the drear
December mists—

that tend to tax
the Scrutinists
of Rue de l'Ouest—

deliquesce,
diaporesis
disappears.

His gazetteer
is clear. His lens
as lucent as

his samovar
(or Heidegger's
late glosses are),

he is aware:
the Tirich Mir,
although it shares

amphimacers
with Hindu Kush,
cannot compare—

it is a mere
particular,
a part, a single

peak and not
at all The-All,
The-Vast-And-Versal-

Mountain-Chain-
Of-Solitude-
And-Grey-Moraine

the name of Hindu
Kush can claim,
the name that can

attain, sustain
(or so Soudaine
Souplesse, whenever

pressed, maintains—
and Angélique
Abrí agrees)

the Great-Gestalt-
Of-All-Gestalten,
Arabesque-

Of-Arabesques—
beneath the heavens'
zafferness.

HONEY-SOIT SAMBA

As if a rufous dawn—
    or citron or persimmon—
    ex tempore had risen
and, having risen, driven
    the tenebrae from shores,
    the subfusc from the caverns,

or as a sudden lantern
    that lights a darkened tundra—
    so would the *savantasse*
on his divan have dreamt
    the awning rolling back
    on a waxed samba floor

whereon a waitress wore
    pearlgrey chinchilla drawers
    that bore both *H* and *S*
as monogram—upon
    the left—for Honey-Soit,
    a recent alias.

And even as she pours
    from a mauve samovar,
    dispensing every-part
of *Come, Ye Sons of Art,*
    across the languid aisle
    of Langerhans, she trips

in low relief and strips,
    imperturbable. Musil
    laces out a cruel
triple. Musial
    plies his novel. So
    insists the Ugaritic

radio. That is, if
    he can hear: he has
    a fountain in his ear.
The city is South Orange,
    Sandusky, or Pyongyang,
    or under Tirich Mir—

but in another year.
    He can't remember which.
    His lexis has the itch.
He strums his gazetteer.
    The waitress has the shakes.
    The rufous awning rips.

The citron samba lifts
    the *savantasse*. He drifts
    upon an almadía,
a prahu, praam, proa,
    caramoussal, caracore—
    beside the Nenuphars

on unobtrusive waters.

BOATSONGS

The unobtrusive waters fade.
The *savantasse* awakes. Day breaks
into the hemisphere of light
a lantern casts. Both lights incite
the squinting *savantasse*. He tries
to gloss the writhing inks inscribed
upon the scroll of lithe Wen Tong.
(Its rhomboid waits somewhat beyond
the cracked carafe.) He sees what some
see as *The Cliffs of Tendai-San*
Seen From a Boat Returning North,
though others say the river drawn
within that scene is nothing more
than Seine between two Sinic shores—
a metamorph. However blear
his foveae, this much is clear:
the calligraphs that flank the scene
allow the *savantasse* to read
and, as he reads, to overhear
and, as he overhears, to grasp—
while reaching for his cracked carafe—
these three discrepant epigraphs:

Returning by Boat on a Cold River (1)

ONE

The sages squat upon the rock.
    The rock is gray above the stream.
    The sages fish for cyprinoids.
    Their nets are meshed with canny nodes.
And when a soft-finned carp is caught,

the sages scurry on the rock:
    they thank the current and the knots
    in all the network that was wrought
    by those who never squat in thought
above the prepossessing rush

of waters carrying the caught
    to those who catch but know remorse
    at having caught and at the thought
    the river will erode (as talk
erodes—in time—a text) their rock.

TWO

Yet those who disentwine and fret
    and fray the mesh of fictive nets,
    who try the truth of every warp,
    whose one beatitude is doubt,
have asked: Would apathetic carp—

whose rage is rest—seek or accept
    an unenlightened habitat
    where seaward, sleepless waters press—
    much like uninterrupted text—
without cesura, sabbathless?

THREE

Therefore the boat—if boat there was—
    from which a baffled eye had dropped
    its tangents toward a school of carp
    and sages—never was embarked
on a cold river returning north,

but lingered on a languid lake
    and saw no Scrutinists who squat
    on somewhat aphanitic rock
    but on a paralimnion
that bore their glutei with soft

and sedentary green that seemed
(as Scrutinist and carp were caught
    in nets that light alone had wrought,
    leaving intact what it had touched)
to need no thought, no scurrying.

Returning by Boat on a Cold River (2)

Who are the sedentary ones
   among the scurrying shipmen?
   One man, two women—seen from shore
   through bitter mists: His wife? His daughter?
   Or is he widower? And these
   a sister and a mother? Or

is he a man who lives in two

   devotions, in the double truth
   of those who wed but—wedding—know
   the heart may need anaphora;
   and—knowing that—can shun despair,
   despite the cold upon the river,
seeing they return together?

Returning by Boat on a Cold River (3)

And even as the boat advances
north and vast and tacit forests
cast their stillness on the waters,

I see—despite the late-November
mist depicted on the river-
banks—the branches of a larch.

Beneath a rough-winged sparrow's nest,
recumbent on a narrow branch—
the boulders, brambles, yarrow, grass.

Upon this last, the hoarse savant.
But he does not recline. He stamps
the saraband of the reprieved,

delivered from his death by ten
parts of speech (that interrupted
when the surreptitious forests'

acquiescent perjuries,
the given guile, the guile received,
had silenced him) before—again

and finally—he finds, beneath
the boulders, brambles, yarrow, grass,
the larches and the sparrows' nests

(observed upon the riverbanks
when boats, returning north, advance
across the late-November mists),

the last, intransigent divan.

Two

THE AYRES OF THE RESTLESS *SÉDENTAIRE*

AN AYRE OF OTHER YEARS

For years on end the *savantasse*
had earned his bread by labor at
his diligent delights and tasks,

nuances of the most exact
alliances of white and black:
the labors of the typograph.

And some contend he found his *ens*
in sarabands of ems and ens
that, even as they dance, depend

on Unrelenting-Measurement,
and in a lens attentive to
the calculating derringdo—

on the dispassionate trapeze
of white—by dark and ardent inks
that, for their own survival, need

discriminating symmetries,
appropriate proximities,
and delicate dexterities—

in brief, The-Wholly-Accurate,
The-Equilibria-That-Rack,
The-Craft-Of-The-Commensurate.

But when—for years may alter ends
that animate the ligaments,
the tendons, and additaments

of *triste chair* and muddled *mens*—
his lens immoderately bent
upon The-Measureless instead,

he knew there was no frontispiece
or colophon that might appease,
and found his appetite decreased,

and left the craft that once had fed
with bread (and rice and kidney beans—
and buoyant purple aubergines

that animate all ratatouilles
along the languid Rue Lebouis)
and went the way of penury,

the very path that—some say—meets
The-Measureless, if only one—
however hungry or undone—

can recognize the intersection.

THE SHELL OF SAINTE-ADRESSE

ONE

That Shell he held at Sainte-Adresse,
  that Shell whose canticle caressed
  his ear as he construed the flecked
  and foaming tan of wrack and red
  of dulse in deft windscripts and drifts,
  the dance of the discarded drafts
  the seas of Sainte-Adresse bequeath
to lonely tidal exegetes,

to that uneasy *sédentaire*
  who left his bare divan to share
  abundant sands, to read a strand's
  hendiadys of sea and land,
  to find, on fathoming the web
  of shadows cast across an ebb
  by tower, cloud, or tall *falaise*,
the rarest Shell of Sainte-Adresse

(or was it Wimereux? or Sète?
  or Cabellou—where he construed?
  What names, what fallen grains confuse
  his hourglass? Can Sainte-Adresse
  withstand the swash of Arromanches,
  the ebb of Brest, the avalanche
  of Chaillevette in one obsessed
by every tidal consonant

and vowel he met—one who had clasped
    along the island strands of Yeu,
    the limit lands of Le Pouldou—
    a *savantasse* whose steps had set
    the pensive prints of soaked sabots
    on sands more numerous than snows,
    who hungered after many shells,
and, where he hungered, always held?) . . .

that Shell his hands had only left
    when night announced the last express
    returning to l'Impasse de l'Ouest
    and hurried him away, had led
    what music of The-Measureless,
    what measure of The-Fathomless,
    what shadowed quays, what fear, what need
into the haven of her lied?

No Baltic brouhaha, no tense
    tamasha of the Indian
    Ocean, no lust to storm that must
    deform the bright Tyrrhenian
    when lash of the libeccio whips
    and even Metamorphosists—
    left derelict—resignedly
shipwreck in shapeless reverie,

had echoed when he held that Shell
   and heard her murmured canticle.
   In her there lived another lied—
   not surge that seethes against a quay
   or shoal so savagely that we
   lose hope of helm and harboring,
   but other tide, an other sea,
the wave of *pacem sabbati.*

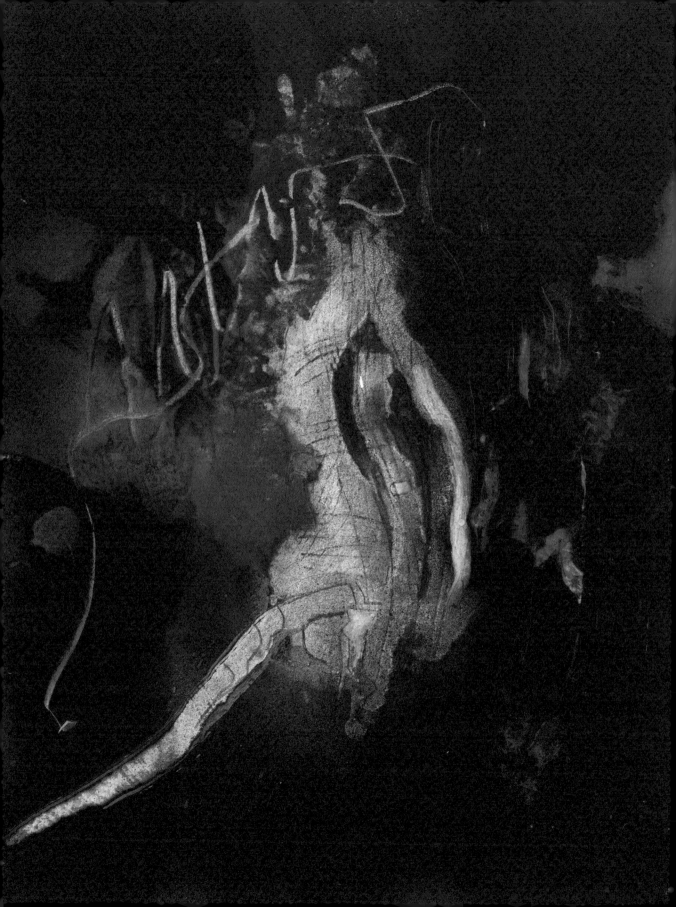

TWO

And with the wave within, what sound
   without might weave the words to which
   that Shell responds (should one insist
   on naming her, as Scrutinists
   will do when drab of winter mists
   deprives their eyes of tidal script,
   of shoreline serpentines and drifts,
confining them to pale pastis

or pipes of bland kinnikinnick
   or else—should shuttered rooms withhold
   the world, but not nine folios—
   to atlases that sail their shelves
   like nine impatient caravels
   that carry The-Ineffable
   until that cargo leaves their hold
and finds The-Name-That-Can-Be-Told)?

Was she a *Trunculariopsis*
   trunculus, Smooth Artemis,
   or Oval Venus, Lurid Cowrie,
   Slipper-Limpet, or—quite simply—
   a Shell that was as well content
   to be a common Wentletrap
   or bear a stammering, redundant
name Linnaeus fashioned when

he was intent on repetends—
    the *Clathrus clathrus*, just as if.
    bereft of the repetitive,
    that Shell might never—on the sands
    of Sainte-Adresse, where tides have swept
    and strewed. but then inclined to ebb—
    find *amador* who, when he clasps
again, again, and murmurs *Clath-*

rus clathrus as he seeks the path
    where each caressive act enacts
    fidelity, would stay and keep
    what he had heard and held, not leave
    that Shell beneath the preying reach
    of Glaucous Gulls' bulimic beaks
    along benighted sands—but be
The-Unrecanting-*Amador*,

Her-Firm-Seigneur, Her-Cynosure,
    The-Tutelary-Murmurer,
    who never would desert her for
    the night express to Saint-Lazare
    or any Gare that swept him far
    too far from her and from the four
    long syllables with which he called
upon—and then beyond—her shell?

THE AYRE OF ALBION

ONE

Again he laced his wordsworths on.
Again he paced with pilgrim haste
across a London slow to wake.

Against the gustings of a grim
northeaster from the fens, upwind
he reached the bridge. Again he waits

for sun reborn to answer one
who journeyed here with lens that longed
for one unhesitating dawn

to steep in splendor, touch with calm,
the very heart of Albion:
the Thames and towers, temples, domes—

the human dwelling earth reveals
when rays of grace incline to heal
the vision and the visible.

But when his dogged lens had gleaned,
in fourteen dawns through which he leaned
upon Westminster Bridge, no scene

whose claim or title could have been:
Firstlight-That-Guides-The-Gazing-Soul-
To-See-The-Parts-And-Sense-The-Whole,

when all that answered his eye-reach
were spectral skies as indistinct
as palettes plied by those who think

there is no tint of truth in inks
of unadulterated hue,
he ripped to shreds his passe-partout—

a perishable pèlerin
alone in an unlikely land,
far from his affable divan,

his hasty haversack in hand
and, in his heart, the wish that he
had heeded Enthymeme when she,

some seven nights before the day
on which he left for London, scanned
his prayer-rug from Kirsehir

and, after murmuring a prayer
for Channel-Crossers, sighed: «Do stay.
No soul, however unallayed,

need seek its peace north of Calais
or south of Porte de Vanves. To stray—
Pascal had warned—is to be prey».

One earring fell. But no delay
could interrupt as she arrayed
the disconcerting *vérités*

that love and thought can hone when they
would exorcise or hold at bay
our yen to yaw and drift away:

«What Dereliction and Dismay,
what God-Forsaken-*Coup-de-Dés*,
Stale-Loaves, Stale-Lust, Pale-*Pis-Aller,*

Ennui, Debris, Cloacae, Thugs,
Fiascos, Filthy-Puddles, Sulks,
Dunghills, and Rifled-Steamer-Trunks,

Disgrace, Disparagements, Repulse,
and Mormoluches and Hoodoos loom
when one abandons one's own room!»

Here she surveyed his samovar
and, taken by his tea, she had
allowed her damask voice to add:

«Hotels and hydrofoils are fit
for those whose haversacks still itch,
who need to mate with the makeshift,

who would betray their *vrai* surtout
and wear a world that does not suit,
and—so misfit, their pleats amiss—

would lust for dunes past Hindu Kush
where burakhans of dust confuse
the passe-partouts of the footloose,

or sled to sleepless bivouacs
by night on northern nunataks
where Stormont-Murphy Arctic Stoves

may scorch sabots of those who rove
in hope of finding on a floe
what may be better left unknown.

Yet even he who seems most bent
on pilgriming can still relent,
can shun the yen to leave his den,

can hum sequestered ayres, prepare
the bread of angels in his lair.
I merely mean that Baudelaire

(and—after all—his *fleurs du mal*
were often watered by Pascal)
conceded: 'Lovers and savants

and cats can consummate their wants
in sedentary quarters. All
can be construed when shutters fall,

if one has vigilant *prunelles*
that can detect, define, sustain
the flame of science and the flame

of *agapē*—clairvoyant rays
that darkness in a dwelling place
provides—austere and fervent space'».

TWO

Then, still along the bridge, his *mens*
retrieved some twenty tercets he
received from Enthymeme when she

(while buttoning her bayadere—
whose green and azure stripes enhanced
the light his rhomboid lantern cast)

had quested though her *Calendar-
Of-Seated-Spirits*, souls whose *chair*
did not hold cheap what is most dear,

and read: «Kant found his Demiurge,
his vast *Vernunft*, his feisty *Burg*,
while visa-less in Königsberg:

ignoring passport photographs
and wiles of wanton atlases
with white vignettes of winter steppes,

he never stared at mezzotints
that emphasize the slender limbs
of siren yews and sandaracs

of forests that delight, distract,
but, in the end, can only damp
the lamp of *Pflicht* and leave us lax—

he never boarded blue couchettes
at *Bahnhof*s with beguiling tracks
where night express departs in quest

of pusztas, *playas*, soft savannas,
or a stagnant, dark laguna's
unforgiving gondolas

wherein a man may ride beside
Oblivion but wake to find
himself incurably supine,

alone with his *Einbildungskraft*,
his will undone and weak as wax
when Honey-Soit renews attacks

or Nenuphars who tend to bend
crouponduleusement again
return, each with the yens of ten.

His *echt* sabots refused to rove
to lemon trees below the Po,
to willows where Ticino flows,

or to the white of almond groves
beside a golden telamone
that grieves within its fallen stone,

to arbors underneath the cone
of Etna, where the light that glides
across the latices of time

entwines the mind in tangled vines,
in trellises of tenebrae
and of the brightness that can blind.

And no sabot of his was known
to stagger in a nomad coma
across the paving-stones of Lucca,

where just four notes of *Nessun dorma*,
erupting from a shuttered window,
can shower far more magma than

Vesuvius or Etna can—
reducing us to babbling dust,
incapable of Turning-Back,

uncertain where That-Back was at,
forgetting even those who packed
with *Gugelhopf*s and tenderness

the hasty haversack we clutched—
with friends embracing us—at dusk
on our departure day. In sum:

he shunned the horizontal paths
of earth, that stretch but cannot grasp:
he stared instead where, overhead,

within the dark beyond his ledge,
the fires of familiar stars,
the flares of Deneb and Altair,

were like the Lanterns-Of-The-Law
the heavens keep and heaven gives:
without, within—the light that lives».

THREE

So Enthymeme had deemed. And Maud
Maraud, with overdue regard,
deferred, concurred. And even Frau

Perforce, although—or else because—
she chose to leave her native Rhine
by way of cold couchette to find

near serpent Seine a hearth that stood
for Every-Warmth-From-Which-She-Would-
Not-Budge, averred as much. And now—

as he retreats from Albion,
his haversack still weighted down
with fourteen Unavailing-Dawns—

the *savantasse* remembers how
Perforce had once (while taking stock
of sedentary hollyhocks

and winter melons she had sown
when Mon Parnasse became her own)
allowed her words to pause and watched

the *savantasse* (restored to *vis*
that he had lost in his pastis)
assault her citron torte—before

it cooled—with every hunger dusk
incites in those deprived of thought;
then, having paused, Perforce had taught:

«Despite the meager light that must,
when All has beckoned us, obstruct
the view from Mont Parnasse at dusk,

if we revere as our most dear
allies the gods who guard The-Near,
who keep our home and heart, our Here,

then mind may find the apt design,
the mortar and the trowel whereby
its reverie can edify

the candid condominiums
with blue desidiabulums
and versatile gymnasiums

where Unimpeachable-Rabbis,
The-Open-Eyed, The-Guides, The-Hives-
Of-Honey-Be, The-Clarified,

can—disembodied—exercise
their hammerblows of The-Unheard
to pulverize The-Carnal-Word,

their thuds of fore- and afterthought
to drub the tenebrae to nought,
and—after afterthought—can plot

their desideribilia,
their radishes and replicas,
their fictions as elysean

as succulent, gargantuan
persimmons, purple aubergines,
Ur-melons, mighty mangosteens,

antimonies and kidney beans
and lentils, then retire in-
to unencumbered patios

where Cogito can cut to size
its disembodied appetite
for delectatiunculae

(the fever that fulfilled the mind
when it was sapling, neophyte,
in need of gymnasts as rabbis)

and be its own replete rabbi—
whose parapegms decline to writhe,
whose similes need never strive—

and gaze at last at its lost prize,
the paramour it had denied,
the *amadou* who does not ride

realia, but walks beside—
Beholder and Beheld in one
embracing condominium».

Then, as she cleared the plate her torte
had graced, Perforce allowed her gaze
to tell the *savantasse* that he—

or any other nomad—drawn,
or commandeered, to slog at dawn
beyond his own arrondissement

to see the splendor earth reveals
when rays of grace incline to heal
the vision and the visible,

had best elect a promenade
to sun reborn on scrubbed facades
of Saint-Sulpice or Saint-Germain

or to the windows of Poilâne
to scan the spheres and octagons
of morning loaves of bread instead

of staggering, with wordsworths on,
to meet the mists of Albion's
forsaken frigidarium.

THE ODE OF THE SCUFFED SABOTS

ONE

The undemanding afternoon
   (the jets of sun that warmed his tan
   tarboosh, his jacaranda, and
   the solitary almond branch
   that overlooked the dormant oud
   and devious charanga flute
   that flanked his fallible divan)
   incited him outdoors and soon
his scuffed sabots had helped him speed

beyond the languid Rue Lebouis—
   until he met l'Impasse de l'Ouest,
   impenetrable cul-de-sac
   no *savantasse* has ever passed.
   His West effaced, he faced the East
   but saw the Tour impeding that.
   Denied, deprived, his compass fashed
   and feized, disseised and bilked, bereft
of all but North and South, he sat

upon The-Ground. Though Paraphrasts,
   impatient of the imprecise,
   an itch they share with Neophytes
   (wherefor conniving odes insist,
   as part of their astuter stichs,
   on minims of meticulous
   vignettes and haptic evidence
   to quiet those who tend to wot
and ween by touch and eye and not

by way of cochleae) attest:
      The *savantasse* had never sat
      upon The-Sad-And-Solemn-Ground
      Where-Seed-Is-Seldom-Cast-Or-Found-
      And-Only-Boulders-Can-Abound
      but on an unbecoming bench
      of rough wrought-iron near a fence
      fashioned of that same element—
both bench and fence erect and yet

defaced by paint that, although patched
      and dappled by discrepant flecks,
      still manifested that, when fresh,
      its color must have been akin
      to greygreen of decrepit grass
      or greenishgrey of stone and moss
      of pedestals in public parks
      that, through the dank December dark,
when turf is sodden, trunks are stark

(and only dripping Connoisseurs-
      Of-Clouds-And-Sloven-Fog are sure
      to pace the paths and parse the parts
      of stratocumulus), support
      the effigies of Joans of Arc
      and sundry Louises, Lothairs,
      and Pippins, Charleses, Hughs, Clotaires,
      and Chilperics—the Bald, the Fair,
the Bold, the Bad, the Debonair

the Hammer, and the Stammerer,
    the Fat, the Mad, the Fifth, the Fourth,
    the Saint, the Affable, the Short,
    the Bruiser, and the Blind—embarked
    on somber stallions as they part
    for unperturbed celestial parks
    or for the dun Musée de l'Homme
    (whose Ragged-Curators admit
that, while some aeons have been spent

on its embellishment, but one
    of its disheveled wings is done:
    The-Inconclusive-Atrium),
    or for The-Indistinct-Precincts,
    whose pensive premises provide
    unending dusk, the leafless time
    that Shamans-Of-Sheol assign
    to vanquished minds who still would ride
the plains of loss with steelgrey pride.

TWO

But whether he had sat upon
   The-Solemn-Ground or on The-Un-
   becoming-Bench whose rough wrought-iron
   discomfits any nates that wait,
   deprived of grace but in the state
   of faith or hope—or states of both—
   of conjuring a path that crept
   or—more imperiously—swept
across l'Impasse de l'Ouest, he wept

upon the spatial indigence.
   The-Interdict-Undue-Unjust
   whereby a cul-de-sac concocts
   a brew of bitter rue to balk
   a *savantasse*, although his scuffed
   sabots had—scrupulously—not
   presumed—this afternoon—to trot,
   trudge, luff, lurch, shove, yaw, scud, subsult
beyond his own arrondissement:

he had not tracked The-Tousled-Ox;
   adored The-Overarching-*Vache*,
   descended into dens and dark
   retreats beneath the Rue Descartes
   to share a subterranean
   tisaine as Maud Maraud explains
   that nothing is denied to us
   once we have quaffed The-Fathomless-
Carafe-Of-Neither-Nor-And-Nought;

he had not climbed the steps of thought—
   or escalators that rebut
   the hundredweights of human dust—
   to taste the tortes of Frau Perforce
   and listen as her precepts course
   like flashfloods or a tidal flux
   across the sands of Is and Ought;
   nor, after tortes and afterthoughts
as well as intricate retorts

(designed by Frau Perforce for those
   who find her *claritas* too close
   to truth to suit their nakedness
   in lieu of their obtuse surtouts
   or other swaddling clouts they choose
   to fend against Aporias-
   As-Chill-As-Bristling-Boreas),
   had he saluted all she said
as unequivocally *echt*

and most astute but hard to use
   unless one were less circumspect
   than he had been compelled to be
   because of tangled ancestry
   (paternal and maternal lines
   where vowels and consonants are twined
   can garnishee lucidity)—
   to which her one reply would be,
«Until new birth has set you free . . .»

Nor had he wended west to watch
    disconsolate Schwarzseher walk
    his dog through distant hedges fraught
    with evidence of hollyhocks,
    hippocrépis, and rampant phlox
    and even the ebullience
    of dandelions that disconcert
    the darkness of Schwarzseher so
with their elated yellow haloes;

nor, venturing past Porte de Vanves,
    had he explored the walks of Bois
    de Meudon, where a warm bourgeoise
    may re-emerge among the boughs
    of sycamores as Honey-Soit
    or, failing that, as Final-Cause:
    instead, his promenade had sought
    an unassuming rhomboid course
across the scarps of Mont Parnasse.

THREE

He wept—and, while he wept, rehearsed
 the words Pascal asserted first
 in sixteen-twenty-three, when he
 imbibed the bane of birth: We brew
 wormwood and rue when we eschew
 our worn *paillasse,* our samovar,
 our warm divan, our oud, our Our—
 or even leave our door ajar,
for Whirliwhaws-That-Wait-Beyond-

Our-Window-panes may cozen us
 to limp or lurch from verst to verst
 of *rues* that run like rivulets
 but die into disconsolate
 wanwoods, wanchance, or sumps that tend
 to swamp the earth with fetid fens,
 or velds and rands where brambles, grass,
 and mulga scrub annul our tracks
in vast and versal culs-de-sac.

Or, less laconically: All
 can be foreshadowed in the scrawl
 of lamplight on and in Four-Walls
 or light of sun as long as it
 would visit us and not insist
 upon enticing us to it;
 in sum, we need the *vis* to sit,
 to shred our gazetteers, to bid
our soul—Be still, stay home, and mull.

Yet having had their fill of dull
    meandering of light on walls
    at which in vain they squinted, scowled
    with cilia and foveae,
    intrepid canaliculi
    and everglaring glands of Moll,
    zonules of Zinn, and the canal
    of Petit—parts the prescient eye
deploys in trying to descry—

attaining nothing for their pains
    except the need (once they'd relieved
    their lagophthalmia with leaves
    of euphrasy, fomented in
    rosewater, fennel, camphire, and
    two drams of tutty, twice a day,
    applied while warm) to stare again
    with bulbs bedimmed and baffled lens
from sagging *chaises* or blear divans,

some Paraphrasts would paraphrase
    another version born of Blaise,
    whom they translate in haggard haste
    and take to mean that, having seen
    the shadow and construed the glow,
    he peered above and pored below,
    he saw The-Ceiling, saw The-Floor,
    he saw that solitude sees more
than just Four-Walls: it sits in Six-

Plane-Surfaces-Behind-A-Door—
 and there installed, the soul may well
 explore its prayer rug, may dwell
 on The-Design-Of-Its-Despair,
 may, as it stares, become aware
 that since, apart from parts, The-All
 is, on the whole, impalpable,
 who only trusts what he can touch
condemns himself to know not much.

FOUR

He wept, yet having wept, he leaned
    like a despondent tower, bent
    on words that might erect, redeem;
    and so inclined, he called to mind
    that time, nine weeks ago, when he,
    leaving the eaves of Angélique
    Abrí's retreat on Cherche-Midi,
    allowed the arc his eyes described
to intersect a passerby.

(Her hair was long and to the ground,
    the length that served a Mélisande
    when she assuaged her Pélleas,
    her tresses drowning his distress
    as in a sweet infiniteness—
    the length that Venus lavished when
    she saw her son—a widower—
    undone by war and waves, and tore
aside her mortal veil, and wore,

for him, her goddess-gown, the Ur-
    Omen that many men implore
    whenever shipwrecked on strange shores—
    though «many men» must needs except
    Pascal, that *virginum ultor,*
    who knew indeed there a *coeur,*
    but held that heart had need of more
    than mothers on a shoreline or
a brother's wife beside a well.)

For he had heard that passerby
        confide (or had she just implied?):
        «Not even Enthymeme denies
        that Leopardi may have sighed:
        'Pascal had paid too high a toll
        for board and bed in Port-Royal's
        preoccupying cubicles;
        no mind need be confined to soar
into infinity.' Outdoors,

        «in eighteen-nineteen, on a slope
        where he had climbed to lone repose
        by way of his astute sabots,
        as he reclined behind a hedge
        with nothing more than fifteen taut
        hendecasyllables he'd brought
        along to mutter when distraught,
        the man from Recanati met
infiniteness's vast sweetness:

        «the space no shape can subjugate
        and no horizon implicate,
        before-beyond the company
        of ancestors and progeny,
        eternity, the centuries,
        the silences—immensity,
        which he then likened to a sea
        where, in the waves of simile,
he seemed to shipwreck buoyantly.

«But, on the other hand, Pascal
    insisted, 'Speechless space appalls,'
    and shipwreck never held him thrall:
    his Deity was not The-All
    of zaffer skies and zaffer seas
    with their abyssal mysteries
    and gliding teleostei,
    Impassive-All of vendavals,
of tramontanas, mad mistrals,

«of dark Haversian canals,
    monsoons, simoons, and föhns, the fall
    of leaves and green replenishings,
    of rivers, rocks, galactic dust,
    and nunataks and pestilence:
    immensities—unsuffering—
    that cannot answer any plea
    but terrify us silently
or magnify by murmuring».

FIVE

So can an afternoon harass
    a savantasse who walks and asks
    for anodynic armistice,
    discreet release, a brief surcease
    from indigest and unappeased
    aporias that ape the tasks
    of Alexander-The-Sleepless
    (whose cilia were so obsessed
by quaeres that they never met).

So did that afternoon undo
    a soul who simply asked for truce,
    a rest for his forwandered flesh,
    for stiff sabots, for stiff distress
    an overwrought astragalus
    endured at every step that meant
    to find no more than mere content
    among the palpable facades
that harbor no perturbing gods.

FOUR PHANTOMS FROM THE FAR SAVANNA

An other afternoon. But this
not lit by sun. Past Saint-Sulpice,
then west on Rue Saint-Dominique,
at quays that wear the mist as if
that grey *gilet* were meant to fit
November mourning vanished gifts
along the leafless Invalides,
he meets the Seine. He crosses it.
Beyond the Passerelle, the thick
brouillard denies an edifice
contours. His scuffed sabots have come
upon the dun Musée de l'Homme.
He lingers in the atrium.
He hears the dark, erratic hum
of the unborn. He hears Chopin's
fountain offering his ears
an ayre of *triste chair*. He hears—
within the walls where man is stored
along converging corridors—
the cry of one conquistador
and then the howl of one pogrom.
He sees a famished Tartar feed
on cedar nuts and honey, sees
a Pima feed on pemmican.
He hears the double-headed drums
of shamans and the motley tongues
of angry men at Shinar and
a reconciling Targuman.
He sees Ulysses on the sea
of Acis, and Penelope,
whose doing is undoing. He

can see a mask that mimes the One
who, although colorless, can breed
both light and dark, who, vomiting
the sun and sundry animals,
engenders sons and cities, walls
and wives. He sees a woman weave
a rug in Kirsehir, and he
can see a Dogon rider come
from far, an interloper on
the plain of Troy. Returning home,
his steps are wandering and slow.
He rests, beyond his threshold, on
his worn divan. At last he scans
his plot of green linoleum.

That plot of green extends. He can
divine savanna-green grasslands
(perhaps the land Wen Tong had meant
when—with a brush that would entrust
to surfaces the colors of
our griefs, defeats, and loves—he lent
his greenest gouache to four brief scenes:
broad grasslands and a nameless stream).
And hearing what he sees—as one
may do when dusk is opportune—
he hears *Four Phantoms from a Far
Savanna* chanting things that are
when fingers find the first sitar
(as well as things that were or could
have been had we caressed the oud
or plied the long charanga flute)

and, nearing something understood,
allows no waking to intrude,
no gorgon eye to intervene
as dream delivers him to dream:

1. The Chronicles

Today I cannot keep the tallies: I
    am tired of telling reckonings that lie
    beyond the banks a man can track (the past—
exhausted abacus—has cracked). I must
    record the near, the here: the Targuman
    (his days embraced one fate: to comprehend—

and mend—the mesh of severed parts of speech,
    that tribe might speak to tribe beyond its reach)
    is at the end of his interpreting.
These final weeks, the compound is enlarged;
    and even from the farthest provinces—
    where women work as warriors—the mourners

bring their despair. And I cannot decipher
    the murmuring of my own memories
    against their sawtooth cries. He dies among
uproar, his sheltered body bound in white
    despite the motley wools and calicoes
    of strangers: ancient women, men who bore

their years as if they were defiant spears
   as long as praise or desecration could
   be understood—but now are nothing more
than crowd that sweats, a sorry carnival
   of tears and of torn hair. He holds his tongue,
   and not from weakness or from unconcern:

he has no thing to say. I watch his eyes;
   I know their shifting is no journey. I
   have watched his wives, his sons, as if a shadow
of what he is or was might touch their brows;
   but they are shrill, as if their hands held shards
   too jagged to be put together now

or ever. They can only carry scruples
   along the paths that die into the low
   brushwood beyond the villages or perish
within the mudbanks on the river's shore
   or in the reeds that punctuate the waters.
   They do not even ache to keep him whole.

And what I can record will soon be scattered
   or amputated in anthologies:
   milestone markings on a way but never
the way itself. They weep against the weight
   of carrying a single corpse, an all.
   I too must compromise, with chronicles.

2. The Sentence

Then what had entered into him? Was it
the meter that had left him discontent?
Some stammering in the speech of priests? We had sent
him out, well-furnished with black loaves and tart
hackberries for the journey (we had stripped
even the storehouse of the dead in that
parched season of sick crops and barrenness
for beast and man). We gave him cunning maps
drawn by our most exact, most passionate
cartographers.

His trip, far past our grasslands, had gone well.
No raiders, fevers, flashfloods. Uneventful.
The tablets he had gone to fetch had called
for no blood sacrifice, no chieftain's child
or fated wife; in fact, before he had chiseled
and scratched, all they had asked for were a few
more prayers, each night, against the damning drought.
When he was done, «each evening» read «each dawn»;
and, too, he had made the invocations less
redundant.

Was he so set on one appointed time?
Did he distrust—suspect false rendezvous
with High-Ones? Did some demon of revision
overtake him, make him blot the given?
Or was simplicity so dear to him
that all the years he still might count upon
the abacus of his ancestors were
not quite enough to hold his stylus back?
To forge an oracle. The sentence was
inescapable.

Below the straight-edge cliff where he was stoned,
the bees, that alter into sweetness, drone.

3. The Invaders

We were their subject race.

The invaders
travelled inland from the far dunes
of their first home
that edged the turbulent waters.

They cut the girdle of our forests,
reached our grasslands, overcame us.

They introduced the abacus,
tobacco plants, The-Tousled-Ox,
sleep in the afternoon, the arts
of healing, and divorce.

We had no complaints.

Their pay was good;
their gods
and their astrologers
agreeable.

It is not easy to content a people:
all things considered, they meant well.

But then, one day—the moon
marking with a gash that seemed a wound,
the thirtieth month of the thirtieth year
after the Blessed Conquest—
a strange unrest—
longings, new belongings—filled our women.

They hankered after the invaders' chieftains.

One by one, they left our beds
to watch the river
that flowed down to the turbulent waters.

Along the banks, they conjured
the sons that they would bear for the invaders.

We had no choice.

After thirty years of peace,
the surprise was complete
and easy, our rebellion:
the necessary slaughter was soon done.

Now the chieftains lie beneath the waters.

Even the old women can't remember
the face or voice of the invaders.

And sweet is sleep in the long afternoons.

4. *The Wives*

In these long afternoons, I always take
    my rest beside the women's quarters; slats
    of jacaranda screen my eyes; I ache
to hear the laughter of his wives, to gather
    disembodied voices I can clothe
    in mustard, bronze, persimmon calamancoes

until—beneath the dress I have imposed—
    each disembodied voice again takes flesh
    and waits where a savanna finds the edge
of waters unperturbed: the only shadows
    are cast by random reeds across the flow
    or by the suasive wives I have invoked.

At times I keep their bodies nameless and
    at times I call on names I have not heard;
    the bite is best when each divines herself:
erect, upon all fours, or squatting, or—
    her belly down on the shoreline's olive brown—
    a pliant dune against the patient ground.

My waking is not heavy: I have seen
    both riverbanks and frauen interleave
    the palm-leaf palimpsest upon my knees.
The gods, the demons keep another time—
    the pestilential moment of the mind:
    disquieting, exacting, unappeased

(o Healers who deny the anodyne
   of riverbanks and reeds, who never need
   to dream the dress, the nakedness, the lied,
the laughter of Signora Enthymeme),
   they beat upon my eyes before the dawn—
   the gods who lead from seed to thread to drum,

the lords of incipit and denouement;
   the gods who see me not; and those who ken
   each apprehensive nerve and ligament;
the god who was undone; the one who won;
   the god of gods; and he who knows that none
   acknowledge him, the lord of the unborn—

god by god, at the slate-gray Gate of Phantom.

Three

THE MAIDEN NAME OF FRAU PERFORCE

ANOTHER AYRE OF YEARS

For years on end the *savantasse*
declined to track The-Tousled-Ox.
He was—as we have said—content

to tend his flock of ems and ens:
that is to say, content by day,
for when his ens and ems were penned

at dusk, he punctually paid
a prayer to Aesculapius,
who watches over all who trust

the body to enable us;
and so enabled, he would hunt
for Honey-Soit on Rue Belzunce,

on Rue Bellefond and Rue Abscond,
on all abeyant *rues* beyond
the Seine, in far arrondissements,

in brash Buzeval, blithe Bobigny,
Saint-Ouen, Vincennes, and Rêverie—
since distant revels leave us free

from staggers, sumps, and sundry stours
endured by some or—some say—more
who undertake *jovén* and *joi*

within their own familiar walls
but find that foveae appall
when known to those on whom they fall.

And when the hour of Honey-Soit—
the many joys, the much *jovén*—
was done, the *savantasse* would wend

his scuffed sabots across the Seine
again and, pocketing his passe-
partout, return to Montparnasse,

to rhomboid rooms whereof the rent
that he had spent for years on end
provided him with an address

which few have found and none have kept
at all in mind—videlicet,
the Rue de Galimatias.

His sabots off, his tarboosh doffed,
in blue surtout, he slowly quaffed
his tafia from cracked carafe;

and lest, upon his new *paillasse,*
he were to dream a dream that dreamt
of dim arrondissements that sleep

within a forest far too deep
to let the hunter or his prey,
the thinker or his thought, retreat,

he trimmed his unenlightened lamp,
delighting in the glare it cast,
and, when that wick was spent, would watch

The-Nought but never saw enough
therein to think thereon or pause.
Thus, when—at last—he moved, it was

into l'Impasse de l'Ouest, repressed
cul-de-sac his steps had met
while on a promenade that left

whatever *mens* he had, perplexed:
and there, along a waiting wall—
beneath impassive ivy—he

discovered lower-case graffiti,
which Frau Perforce (or was it Maud
Maraud?) had amiably scrawled:

the predator within his breast
has come to rest: it does not ask
for outlet—only to be fed.

PRECEPTS OF FRAU PERFORCE

i

My maiden name was Claritas.

ii

I married Herr Perforce because
I had to.

iii

But having shared
recumbent cares
and cares erect
with much of Herr
Perforce, I left
him and the Black

Forest.

iv

And when I fled
I made my bed
in cold couchette:
I did not rest

until the lucid
tracks were at

the Gare de l'Est.

v

Then, *jamais lasse,*
I hurried south
to sun bestowed
on paving stones
and warm facades
that solace Mon

Parnasse.

vi

Woodways gave way to *vieux pavés*
and *vieux pavés* to alleyways.

vii

But alleyways soon opened on
the Promenade des Horizons.

viii

I want to help the *savantasse*.

ix

If he would find
The-Tousled-Ox,

he must define
its whereabouts.

x

Infraction of the Law
of Contradiction is
the path of precipice.

xi

The nights of Enthymeme are full
of what may well
appall.

xii

Beware of Nenuphars.

xiii

That fiction so elysean
that truth might live in it as if
it were not makeshift is

abyss.

xiv

A beaten rug sheds slow gold in the sun.

xv

A beaten man sheds blood.

xvi

On Disquisition's-Double-Gong
of sounds unstruck and of struck sounds,
I hear the *savantasse* implore.

xvii

Across the derelict divans,
across the river-banks and beds

of serpent Seine, the paving stones
and palpable facades of Mont-

parnasse, the haunts of Rue Abscond,
and cracked carafes, and yarrow, grass,

and boulders, brambles, and the sands
and Glaucous Gulls of Sainte-Adresse—

the lanterns of Mnemosyne
and shadows of Madame Oublí

contend for Ur-Maternity.

xviii

Only the first has mothered me.

xix

My maiden name
was Claritas.

xx

Muss es sein?

xxi

How shall the precepts be aligned?

xxii

Along the Rue Lebouis—
or even to the north,
along the Cherche-Midi—
to be perforced is simply
to overtake Necessity.

xxiii

Es muss sein.

xxiv

I plant the aubergine
in time

xxv

Tomorrow I shall plant the winter melon.

xxvi

Soudaine Souplesse
is prowler, priestess, and procuress,
nurse and fever—any guise
except the one that might appease.

xxvii

And as for Angélique Abrí . . .

xxviii

Outworn sabots
should be disposed
of.

xxix

La cause des soupirs
est fort differente
de celle des larmes—
but both do harm.

xxx

The paths of galimatias
need never vex
if one is sure

only to cross a carrefour
with nothing more
or less than four

corners.

xxxi

The lens of Greta Lentz
ignores the evidence.

xxxxii

Some—who misunderstand—
contend the sweetest *ens*
must be the Honey-Soit.

xxxiii

But on the Rue Lebouis,
it is the Honey-Be.

xxxiv

Nenuphars
lack nectar.

xxxv

Muss es sein?

xxxvi

Do parapegms need pararhymes?

xxxvii

I have left the Black Forest
behind.

xxxviii

The cap that can withstand the sun's
defiance on the slopes of Mont
Parnasse is not the tan tarboosh:

it is the petasos.

xxxix

Though man may be intent upon
recumbent shells that can suborn
his mantel, he must not collect

the Oval Venus . . . .

xl

. . . . and not let
the *Clathrus clathrus* haunt him yet.

xli

Forgo the sands.
Dispel the shell.

If one's divan
is inland, dwell

there.

xlii

And as for Angélique Abrí . . .

xliii

However tall her bell-
tower, it is
frêle.

xliv

Distrust the shandrydan: it can
collapse before the Rue de Rennes.

xlv

Uff, es ist geschehen!

xlvi

Tomorrow—on
the Promenade
des Horizons—

I mean to plant
the winter melon.

xlvii

The value of odóndonite
is slight.

xlviii

Beneath a staghorn sumac
(or was it sandarac?)

within the distant Black
Forest of Remorse,

I married Herr Perforce.
And even now he soughs:

«I could have done far worse».

xlix

The lens of Greta
Lentz is bent: it
lacks reflectiveness.

l

Though intravenous instruments'
unmediated nourishment
propitiates the passionate,
the *mens* prefers its aliments,
its loaves of rough realia
by way—however indirect—

of villi.

li

The time one spends
in earning bread is
not to be contemned.

lii

To mix as one's insistent inks
pigments of mist and brume, to think

one's brush must stroke as if upon
a noctograph is—so Wen Tong

has taught—not to be thought
productive . . .

liii

. . . whatever
my neighbor,
intruder,
or lodger,
or suitor,
Herr Finster
Schwarzseher,
may murmur.

liv

My maiden name was Claritas.

lv

I was reborn along l'Impasse
de l'Ouest.

lvi

Redundancy can guide the vexed.

lvii

Astonishment is an excess.

lviii

Who can excise excess is blessed.

lix

A samovar is polished best
by lucidness.

lx

The *rues* of Montparnasse
restore the *ruhe* I lost
along the shadowed *strasse*
I crossed with Herr Perforce.

lxi

Pure water on pure ground,
although cast down,
is sound.

lxii

I want to find the *savantasse.*

lxiii

I want to shine his samovar.

lxiv

I want to mend his cracked carafe.

lxv

Adherence to the Law
of Contradiction is

the only staff to keep
that man away from his

abyss.

lxvi

Es
muss
sein.

lxvii

Today—along the Rue Lebouis—
I plant the aubergine
in time.

lxviii

No reproach can rightly
be brought against this world save only
that It is not That.

INTERROGATIONS

ONE

Diderot or did Rousseau?—
so did The-Indecisive probe

the *savantasse,* who—when provoked—
would linger just enough to stroke

the rufous hairs that flecked his taupe
pickerdevant and swear an oath

to honor Frau Perforce with all
the *hyperdulia* the soul

owes to The-Unequivocal
and, as he honored her, to hold

her fiats undefiled (because
the Law of Contradiction was

the only cord to keep a man
away from white abyss), but then

relapsed into reflection on
the worn *paillasse* of his divan

and, to the quaere that was posed
before he had begun to stroke

the rufous hairs that flecked his taupe
pickerdevant, responded: *Both.*

TWO

L'Impasse de l'Ouest had one gazette:
the *Cul-de-Sac*. It often asked:

«Was Alexander-The-Sleepless
but Alexander-Obsequens

whom Frau Perforce, whatever her
demands on tender *amador*s,

had (even in crepuscular
fatigue that follows hard upon

an afternoon with Heidegger's
late lucubrations) found to be

(since he was ignorant of rest
and knew no other pause except

that pause in which he let his head
align with his pickerdevant)

unfailingly compliant?»

THE SYMBOLIC LOGICIAN CURBS HIS DOG

Among the unenlightened mists
    that eddy southward from the sixth
    arrondissement *à l'improviste*,
    when Winter's will is done and *Nichts*
    and dark descension must afflict
    the lamps of Rue Vercingétorix,
    which an Ecclesiastesist
(a dank and dour misogynist
    expatriate, an ex-symbolic
    logician who was not Carnap
    but was not certain he was not—
    despite a passport photograph
    where both his face and paraph were—
    however time had tried to blur—
irrevocably those of Herr

Schwarzseher) often used to curb
    his Dog (that once belonged to Maud
    Maraud and then to Frau Perforce—
    who bartered him away because
    she needed one far less averse
    to hearing her precepts rehearsed,
    a hound more bent on parapegms—
and having appertained to them,
    was never *ruhig* in his yens
    but gnawed at endless sentences
    as if the bones of his intent
    were meant for more than hasty scraps—
    although his gnawing often left
    his long *particula pendens*,
much as *disjecta membra* can

harass astonished *écrivains*—
    or *écrevisses* when torn apart
    by neophytes who never learn
    dismembering is a fine *ars*—
    or narrators too-often stirred
    by tafia or samovars
    with hot tisaines from Tirich Mir
or by the knots of Kirsehir,
    or metaphors discrepant as
    a meteor and nematode—
    that then explode or, lowly, worm
    their way to less-than-nothingness
    or interplanetary dust
    as All is pulverized to Parts
in stanzas pitted with the pox

of pullulating *enjambements*),
    the *savantasse* had overheard
    Schwarzseher murmur as he lurched
    together with his leashed *copain*
    in need of a *vespasienne:*
    «When Faust in us succumbs at dusk
    and Dog reclaims The-*Tiefe-Nacht*,
The-*Nebel*, Nought, Unwashed-Subfusc,
    The-Dun-And-Dirty-Erebus-
    That-Waits-Within-The-Niche-Of-Us,
    the Poodle bays insidious,
    beguiling elegies across
    the tenebrae of Montparnasse
    and—baying—wags its blasphemous
and proud extremity above

the curb of guttered *gravitas*.
   Margaret straddled, Helen raped
   are the revenge the Dog must take,
   hound-tales embarked upon a rug
   that bears whatever Kirsehir
   has dared to conjure in its prayers,
   and more—a carpet borne upon
the breath of Doussa-Donna, Bitch-
   And-Honey-Soit-Within-The-Wish-
   Nightfall-Awakens-In-Our-Niche,
   as—circling thaumaturgically—
   the Poodle (alias *Caníche*,
   Barbéto, Cerberus, *Canis*,
   or *Kelev*) scratches at his only,
lonely ontological itch».

Four

THE HALFWAY HOUSE

THE KNOTS OF KIRSEHIR

Despite its bright *mihrab* and pair
of lithe latchhooks above five stairs,
its rufous wool in double weft,
the hypnagogic cypresses
embroidered in its border, and
the twelve true colors it commands,
with fringes saffron as the sands
when clouds are cleft at Sainte-Adresse
and sun can undertake to bless,

the prayer rug from Kirsehir
is The-Design-Of-His-Despair:

the thought of its one-hundred-twenty-
two-thousand-and-four-hundred knots
entangled in the tortured plot
of every fabricated square
meter mimes his helplessness
within the circumbendibus
of bivouacs among the scarps
and spurs of nights on Mont Parnasse
when soul is stripped of whereabouts.

THE BRANCH THAT BEARS TWO AYRES

ONE

Twice-seven sips
of his
pastis . . .

Nevertheless,
he sees
there is

indeed a vase:
the vase
consists

of sturdy *grès*.
An almond
branch

inhabits it.
The branch
resists.

Above the rim,
it lifts
its limbs.

It flourishes.
It does
not quit

blossoming:
against
the green

linoleum,
its life
is white

offering,
the fairest
leavings

he has
swept away
in years.

TWO

Beneath the clock's divided hands,
when he had quaffed his cracked carafe
and, at the bottom of his glass,

had found the same realia,
the same insolubilia,
the very same *agrypnia*

that plagued before he had begun,
he watched—as one may fasten on
a talisman or angel come

to banish his delirium—
the leavings of the almond branch
along the green linoleum

or on his prayer rug, yet—as
a man whose mind was garnisheed
too long by leafless seasons—asked:

«*Quid deus, unde nives* . . . Whence
the snows? What is the god to which
this branch would bring this offering?»

THE AYRES OF THE OUTWORN

ONE

He had no other place to go.
He let his two dismayed sabots

impel his rhomboid *Cogito*
across the prayer rug; and then,

attentive to the precedence
each sabot claimed as it advanced,

he held that faith preceded hope—
until his days denied him both.

TWO

Beneath a bridge he cannot name
(it surely does not cross the Seine

or span the riverbed between
the cliffs of Tendai-san that seem

to overlook his dark divan
down from the diptych of Wen Tong),

the water thickens, ice is near.
Beyond the river he can hear

no answerer.

THE AYRE OF AND

Disease and its indignities
(the fever, catheters, malaise,
and—diligent at his sickbed—

the needle and the dripping flask
of intravenous instrument
whereby rhe sweet and brine, deprived

of every smell of earth, provide
unmediated aliments;
and stupefactions in his head,

morphine and foul forgetfulness
and muddle, stour, indecorous
brouillard and brume and mess) impede

the rivers of remembrance. And
despite the distant pianoforte,
erupting from the hidden court

(that lies behind the Rue Bellefond's
squat hospital, a halfway house
north of his own arrondissement)

with sostenuto passages
and *aspiratamente* notes,
his will cannot receive, retrieve

that undemanding morning when
Soudaine Souplesse enlightened him:
No fountain found by man so brims

and even in the sécheresse
of silences and doubt can hymn—
as can the fountain of Chopin.

OUT OF HAND

He rode upon a shandrydan.
He read beneath a rufous lantern.

He heard the fountain of Chopin.
He watched the lonely almond branch.

He saw the clock's divided hands
embrace at noon in reverence.

He drank carafes of tafia
and met insolubilia—

but ate the bread of indigence
and dreamed the brow of Greta Lentz.

He walked within his stiff or scuffed
sabots. He thought—but not enough—

of Parts and Alls and what we can
dismember and what cannot be

divided lest the living *ens*
be lost or far from evident.

The hands divide. They cannot grasp.
His sickbed sags on three warped slats.

The gap between his lips is like
a needle's eye, a narrow sigh

through which he threads this coronach:
«My body flanked by barren hands,

my liederbook more leafless than
this charnel-house near Rue Chagrin,

I cannot wake the dormant oud,
not stir the soft charanga flute.

I hear an *orgue de Barbarie,*
a scrannel barrel-organ keyed

to '*Overtures-That-Must-Precede-
The-Black-Gavottes-Of-Frau-Oubli*'».

Five

THE LIEDERBOOK OF SEVEN DEATHS

The Leaves of Absence that Possessed
the Sickbed of the *Savantasse*

THE LIED OF LIBATION

The catabatic autumn rains,
descending waters more arcane
than memorable rivers—Seine
or Meuse—or navigable *rues*,

the atramentous autumn rains,
diluvial against his panes,
beget a Muse, a *vieille ouvreuse*,
primordial Madame Oublí,

too ancient, too peremptory
to let Memoria preempt
her claim to Ur-Maternity.
Her shawl is long and to the ground

across her dark himation—
her salutation has the sound
of shells that harbor shadowed shoals
and rouning waters in their whorls.

The savantasse cannot refuse.
He takes the cup of her tisane—
its *grès* is granitegrey and stained.
Three times he lifts it to his lips.

And at the third the cup is drained.
And no tisane from Tirich Mir
in sedentary samovar,
saguaro brew or pale *pastis*,

no tafia or cannabis
sativa, sutra, psalter, or
assuaging sura offered more
forgetfulness than this. His lips

are acquiescent: *Vieille ouvreuse—*
he murmurs like a voice too used
to vocatives—*O vieille ouvreuse,*
je viens voir ton spectacle noir.

THE LIED OF FRAU OUBLÍ

He ransacks half-a-century
of haversacks and reverie.
He scans the maps and portulans
of shores explored before his lens
was bent on Montparnasse. He sees

the fireworks behind the leaves
of tutelary almond trees
and, when the festal fires are spent,
the undiminished force of red
flambeaus of neon flowering

from ragged quays and—overhead—
the flares of Deneb and Altair
above a tranquil arbor where
a total table has been set—
beneath the pliant trellises

of condurango vines—for chess;
the mate-in-three that—suddenly—
redeems the baffled sacrifice
of tattered pawn, forsaken knight
(as if a fluent angel soared

across a long-beleaguered board
to free a fettered king). But these—
the chess, the lithe phylacteries
of trellises, the seaside quays,
flamboyant neon, almond leaves,

the feast of fireworks—recede,
as if the will to memory
reclined beneath the Absence Tree
and, having slept, awoke to see
the tenebrae of Frau Oublí.

APARTSONG

These distances—that once would prey
as alien marauders or
sporadic scavengers—now stay.

Together with defiant debts
repaid again, again, that yet
coerce, and shame reclaiming more

than intermittent penitence,
and disbeliefs that plead to be
relived, regrieved—these distances

have joined my house of disarray.
They bawl for board and bed. They are
at hand. But I had wanted far

more nearness hoarded, here, beside
the tarnished samovar, the rinds
of aubergines and apples, signs

of taken sustenance—and not
these godforsaken mendicants,
these distances. You are so far.

A LIED OF LIKENESS

The reef. The absence. Each
can serve—to save, to shatter,

or—finally—to stand
and witness what it can

not comprehend: against
the unforgiving azure,

the derelict, past reach,
that sinks—intact and silent.

THE LIED OF LEGAL TENDER

Too many hands had passed it on
to him.
    It had become a coin

adulterated and defaced:
the force—
    inherited from Shem—

to fornicate and propagate,
accumulate,
    propitiate

the gods of grove and hearth and place—
the Lesser gods—
    and then the Great,

who overlook the restive fate
of porous matter
    and of dense,

of rocks—compressed,
of fire—expressed,
    of sin and sudden penitence.

He stopped.
(In litany he'd lost
    his way.) He watched

the tutelary
branches of an almond tree:
    the half sun scrieved

across the leaves,
across the bark.
    He felt the suasive light, a warmth.

But what he wanted
was the dark.
    He counted his remaining force:

the breath, the bread
he might expend:
    the coin he always had contemned.

He saw that it
was counterfeit—
    and yet he held it fast—as if

it had been pure—
for one sure end:
    the bribe he must surrender,

his only
legal tender,
    before he crossed the border

to find the final
fraud, the last
    leaf upon the Tree of Absence.

GARE DU NORD

His north is come. His heart has crossed.
   The gray moraine reclaims his trust.
Within the agitated dusk
   that stirs the south, only his husk

remains—a rudiment—to watch
   the plaintive colors of the clouds,
the flow of frauen, distant shades
   along the rhomboid promenade,

to think the counterfeit of thoughr,
   to love with credible likeness of
desire, to conjure—even touch—
   the body of a girl, enough

   to gift a man with sleep—
   were there no north in reach.

THE LIED OF THE LYING SEAS

As lying seas that bare their tranquil breasts
to heedless mariners and then—relentless—
drive them to loss among the shoals and breakers,

so did the night invite. So Frau Oublí
had offered her *spectacle noir*: and he
forgot the lied of Angélique Abrí,

the testament of Greta Lentz, to see
The-Dalliance-Of-Soul-And-Its-Debris-
Entwined-Upon-A-Divan-Undersea.

Six

THE WOMEN AT THE WINDOW-PANE

THE AYRE OF VERT

December tenth. The convalescent
savantasse no longer writhes:
the phantoms of his own demise,
the deaths received or seized—supine
disease or chosen suicide—

recede. The bed of sickness seems
no last divan. At last he dreams—
but not of soft savanna-green;
the anodynic pulse that beats
from each ascending lid to each

descending lid as tacit sleep
invites the cilia to meet
incites him to the bombazeen
bayadere of Enthymeme
beneath her iridescent earrings'

odondonite, echoing
that most intransigent of greens:
the plains of rice in late July
beneath Vercelli's patient sky,
.   .   .   .   ripening.

IN TOTO

Just as December sun regressed
    behind the jacaranda branch
    that twined across his dark divan
    as if the arms of Greta Lentz
    on metamorphosis were bent,
he thought on Ovid's likeness cast
    in bronze in bright Sulmona, and
    of cunning light on mountain caps,
    of solaces that none can wrest,
    expect, or architect, but one
awaits as will restores itself
    in toto—like the Selfheal plant
    renewing its tenacious bracts
    across the driest field or path—
    or like The-Ox-That-Knows-No-Wrath
returning to the herdsman's staff.

AN AYRE OF APPARITION

Although the dour December mists
that eddy southward from the sixth
arrondissement may interdict
the lamps of Rue Vercingétorix,

they breed in their secretive midst
that force of apparition which
astonished Metamorphosists
are never given to resist

(we are the wax, but not the seals;
the wicks that sputter, not the fuel;
the said, through whom the unrevealed
may murmur but will still conceal).

Thus, when the winter mist descends
the serpent Seine and Rue de Rennes,
then reascends the frozen scarps
of Mont Parnasse, the crass canards

of coarse Iconoclasts contend
that Enthymeme and Greta Lentz,
Soudaine Souplesse and Angélique
Abrí are siren company,

four daughters of the indistinct,
four shadows in a dim precinct.
But souls whom such eidolons bless
(who know that—given to neglect

OVERLEAF: *That Force of Apparition*

or festering or gone to seed—
our needing to adore can breed
distemper, rheum, perplexity,
catarrh, and sullen agony)

confute the crude Iconoclasts'
canards, *bobard*, and blague; and in
defence of shadows, they submit
a witness we cannot dismiss:

the mountain-climbing Florentine
who—on a hillside at whose crest
the Earthly Paradise was set—
in sandals or sabots, had gleaned

that shadows are not shades, that flesh-
and-bone alone can shadows cast.
And from that Tuscan, those who thrive
on writhing winter mists derive

this corollary: Fog that drifts
or eddies southward from the sixth
arrondissement would only give
more life to what already lives.

THE AYRE OF THE ANARCHIC LARCH

Beneath the rough-winged sparrow's nest:
one boulder, brambles, yarrow, grass.
Upon this last the *savantasse*,
recumbent—with Soudaine Souplesse—
reflects on the anarchic larch.

(Whereas the leaves of podocarpus,
possumhaw and eucalyptus,
Sitka spruce and staghorn sumac,
sycamore and sandarac,
tame withy, Tortuosa beech,

and jacaranda never need
to alter—even as they seek
the light above their petioles—
their angle of *intentio*,
no Scrutinist has yet foretold

the quaquaversal larch's yens:
from branch to branch its leaves can tend
askew, awry, erect, anent,
or sly crunodal curves can bend
its penchants unto any end.)

And while the pliant pair assessed
the larch's lithe inventiveness,
did she wear nakedness as dress
while he—in tan tarboosh and vest—
refined his fleshliness? Or she,

a bayadere and zaffer jupe
while he considered in the nude?
Or were they simply two who stood
or sat in mutual undress
or dress (for—some protest—this last

enhances wantonness)? And as
they sat, devising arabesques
(before the ultimate divan
annuls the rites of restlessness—
the patient passacaglia and

the calculating saraband,
the thraws and throes, the helplessness
of man and woman, breast on breast)
did either, none, or both conclude:
Whatever Pascal says, one day

away from Montparnasse in May,
beneath the rough-winged sparrow's nest,
recumbent on the yarrow, grass,
deciphering the furtive larch,
may even cleanse the heart of dust?

THE AYRES OF ANGÉLIQUE ABRÍ

ONE

No woman who, at her departure
northward, can forget: one azure
bayadere and one persimmon

beret; her notes on Saint-Simon;
that flask of Amor Vitae Lemon
Shampoo; *Chamade, Farouche, Vent Vert*

(three phials that might have overcome
the diatribes of the *De Rerum*'s
bitter scribe with their *parfums*);

sunglasses, scratched, tan-violet;
and (on that pinewood half-moon desk
where sudden jets of sun reflect

the days her winter visit blessed)
a single, iridescent earring—
need ever contemplate her being

forgotten.

TWO

The woman who descends the stairs
as if her salutation were

the burning spear, horses of air,
the bread to bless the traveller

who journeyed here from his despair
by way of a clandestine path

and mean expedients—perhaps
forgives the plight of one who lived

as if the plain of Montparnasse
were more than galamatias.

THREE

The swell is soft, the serpents still.
La nuit s'en va, et ses chandelles . . .

He wakes beyond the screech of cats
across the seas of Montparnasse.

The ceiling stretches now intact
above his head, the only bell

he hears: The-Undeniable.
He rises to the syllable

on syllable that beats upon
the unimpatient air as will

a tutelary crane—or angel.

Seven

AFTER THE BRUSH

OVERLEAF: *The Tousled Ox in the Luxembourg*

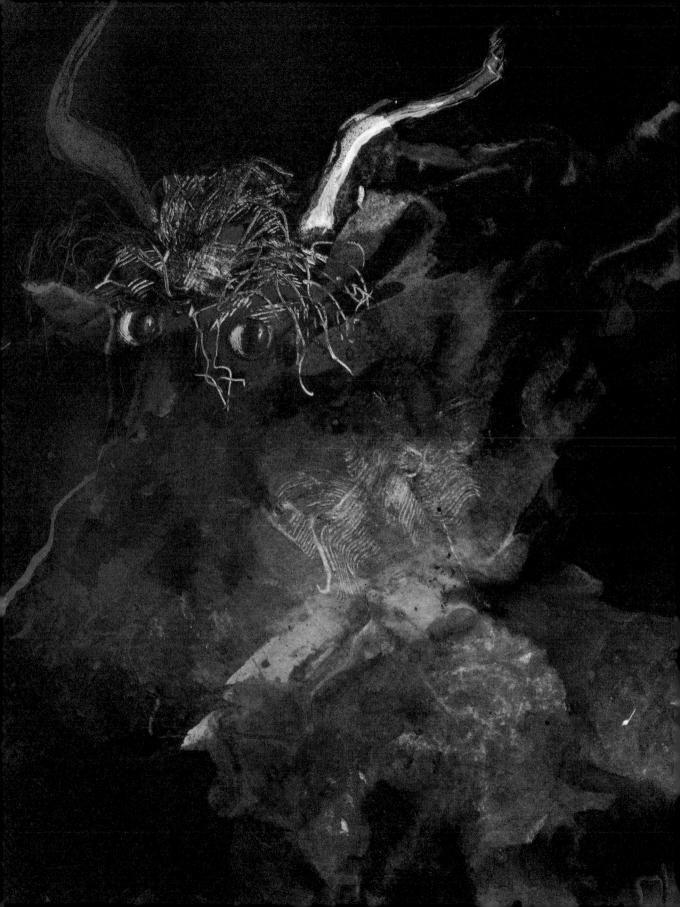

1. The Paraphrasts of Montparnasse

Now, tacit dusk of terminus,
the dusk of the abandoned brush,
possesses the protagonists
as well as worn diaskeuasts;
and That-Which-Has-Been-Told perceives
(despite distraught parentheses)
The-Mute-and-Mitigated-End
envisioned when a rufous dawn—
above a tentative divan—
beheld The-Incipit begun:
in brief, barbituritic dusk
descends upon the *savantasse*
with penetrating evidence
he now is nearer reticence
(the torpor in the cilia,
the *mens* that finds aporias
need not harass, the cigarette
that is the last before the last,
and the penultimate carafe,
the traffic in l'Impasse de l'Ouest
that, for an instant, echoes less
than one belltower to the east
or than the name of Greta Lentz
and face of Angélique Abrí
well-met in murmured reverie)
and tempts the *savantasse* to set
his head upon his torn *paillasse*
and tempts the rest of us to set
aside the dance of variants,

the seeking every slant intent
(and all that may not have been meant)
by lantern light—to wait instead
until new *claritas* is shed
by sun along the Rue Jules-Guesde,
for sleep is meet before—perhaps—
we wake again and, wakened, ask.

But while the *savantasse*, supine
upon his dark divan, aligned
at last with lethargy, may find
in Final-Lines an anodyne,
no Denouement so unadorned—
so fashed and fading, mute and wan—
can quell the Paraphrasts of Mont
Parnasse: as soon as dusk has touched
their cilia, their itch to gloss
(like lust in libertines or monks,
or serpents' need to slough, or just
as zealously as Frau Perforce
impelling precepts in the course
of lowering her love to thought)
reverberates—*perférvidus.*
And thus, with dusk, the Paraphrasts
of Montparnasse would scavenge far;
they rifle every escritoire
beyond the serpent Seine, along
the writhing Marne and Dogne and Yonne,
and when they scent a Colophon
too *fade* or find a feeble *Fin*,
both unappeased and seized, they dun

The-End of any artifex
as if it owed an endless debt
to them and them alone; they stun
The-Denouement with raging rum-
ram-ruf, with boanergic blun-
derbusses, glosses blind as brumes
beleaguering the Rue Pantoum
when autumn clouds *pinarium*s
or (altering similitudes—
for many Scrutinists must do
no less when truth slogs into view
by ways that are not one but two)
as blind as winter gusts that vex
untarnished snows along the tracks
of Gare du Nord or Gare de l'Est
(or any Gare the Paraphrasts
forgather at for night attacks)—
those gusts that, as they wax, vex next
the snows of noble nunataks
above the noble northern floes
and, having harassed there, impose
their dark farrago on the snows
of Snowdon and the snows of prose,
on snows of tors and snows of tumps,
on bluffs, braes, buttes, craigs, knaps, knobs, cloughs,
on any snows that loom enough
across a zaffer azimuth.

And when a Paraphrast is set
to dun and stun and gust and gloss,
to chrónohótonthólogós,

declining to digress, he lets
his cilia ascend, descend,
suspend, perpend, and—brusque—adjusts
the lint on his surtout, the dust
along his frayed tarboosh, reflects
(no longer than a Beglerbeg,
a Boyar-Whose-Bulimic-Urge-
Is-Vaster-Than-Varuna's-Girth,
a Sagamore-With-Major-Thirst,
a Hyperthyroid-Hosopodar,
a Cockarouse or Commissar
would take to drain a samovar
when proffered by a khidmutgar,
or—others add—as quickly as
a Mélisande and Pélleas,
embraced, would take to cry: «At last!»),
then swallows ten successive gasps,
ransacks the flatus for his rasps
and, in despite of phlegm, must ask:

2. Rabbits and Crows in the Night Snow?

«But even as its rhomboid hung
above the devious divan
(whereon the *savantasse* collapsed
when each of his Twelve-Passions and
his legal tender had been spent,
misplaced, or lost, or lent), what did
the Final-Scroll of wry Wen-Tong
depict?

«Was it—as some insist—
A-Fledgling-Metamorphosist-
Returning-On-A-Salvaged-Ship,
A-Leaking-Caracore-That-Bore-
Him-North-Along-A-Cold-River?

«Or did the Final-Scroll construe,
by way of gouaches more diffused,
A-Metamorphosist-Subdued
(his slowed sabots less given to
traversing rivers, straits, and *rues*;
his *triste* chair grown less astute
in seeking southern *amadou*s
beside barbituritic bayou
waters where the white juburu
wades, or in the race to yew
for dalliance on northern dews
with *amadou*s so vigorous
at throe, gambado, lurch, and thrust
that, though incited body soughs
enough, enough, enough, enough,
it knows a semiquaver truce
will let it rise to rush anew
to truth of touch and untouched truths,
the you we name and nameless You),
a man more fashed, far less acute
in stuffing every blue surtout's
last pocket with the passe-partouts
and vigilant charanga flute
and Honey-Soit he used in youth
to sweeten wanderings—one who

(on finding he has faltered far
enough to face a carrefour
of Prayer-Rugs and Barren-Floors,
of Now, Not-Now, and Nevermore,
Gamashes, Galligaskins, Greaves,
Galoches, Spatterdashes, Leaves-
Of-Grass and Leaves-Of-Absence or
of The-Abundant-Escritoire
of Of, of Nothing-But, of Or,
of Goniums and Almost-Gods,
Leviathans and Gastropods
that carambole with Alls and Parts
when Raptus calls for red gavottes
and caprioles, and Grand-Gestalts
and Darting-Doits collide athwart)
declines to dance, declines to cross
that carrefour, declines to rush
to rash gavottes, and seeks a rock
and, having found it, thereon squats
and waits until *That-Red-Debauch,*
*That-Rufous-*Falak-Al-Aflāk,
Descends-To-Grey-And-Denouement?

«Or seated at the southern gate,
where sun may warm the reprobate
until its rays have ceded place
to lines of force from star to star,
like bonds between remotest fires
of distant sons and distant fathers,
was Wen Tong drawn to undertake
a diptych that would adumbrate

the dream of one who cannot wait,
who (when his tafia narrates—
or pale *pastis* insinuates—
damnation, lassitude, and grace)
would plead with trance to tender space
enough for him to meditate
on soft savanna-green or on
savanna-green linoleum
until the walls that wall his *mens*
have fallen, and viridians
become savannas that embrace
eternities *a parte post*
and then *a parte ante*—and,
in his hallucinarium,
sees icons in the atrium
that fronts the long Musée de l'Homme,
four fluent shapes the swift Wen Tong's
savanna-green gouache transformed
to *Phantoms-From-A-Far-Savanna*?

«Or, in despite of what is said,
did Wen Tong's ox-hair brushes end
with just *A-Branch-of-Jacaranda-*
Adjacent-To-A-Possumhaw?

«Or were the final inks of Wen
Tong bent upon profounder green:
The-Unassuming-Lunula-
Beside-The-Torc-And-Fibula-
Above-The-Breast-Of-Enthymeme—
or *Her-Odondonite-Earrings*?

«Or, when his brush had journeyed much
in visibilia and such
invisibilia as brush
and gouache can touch, when he had passed
beyond his *Boulders-Brambles-Grass*;
his *Monkey-Gazing-At-A-Wasp*;
Two-Egrets-And-Three-Mallow-Plants;
The-Fable-Of-The-Cul-De-Sac-
In-Which-The-Tousled-Ox-Is-Trapped;
The-Aubergine-Is-Unabashed;
His-Father-In-A-Brown-Plaid-Cap-
Construes-A-Tattered-Testament;
and *Catching-Catfish-With-A-Gourd*;
The-Tousled-Ox-In-The-Luxembourg;
his sixfold screen of *Nomads-Cranes-*
And-Mendicants-Arriving-Late-
At-Night-Before-The-Northern-Gate;
The-Prepossessing-Widow-Waits-
Beneath-The-Bridge-At-Tendai-san-
To-Hear-The-Fountain-Of-Chopin;
and *Women-At-The-Window-pane-*
Deciphering-Descending-Rain;
his *Wife-Beside-The-Blue-Dordogne-*
Deciphering-An-Only-Son;
his *Son-Beside-The-Green-Garonne-*
Recalls-Four-Lands-He-Has-Called-Home;
The-Silhouettes-Of-Spleen-And-Stealth-
Invade-The-Caverns-Of-The-Self;
No-Fish-No-Bird-Has-Need-Of-Walls;
His-Father-In-A-Prayer-Shawl-
Beseeches-Parts-To-Render-All;

Pascal-Would-Gore-The-Patient-Ox;
The-Ox, Appalled, Has-Fled-The-Stall;
and *Nostrils-Mouths-Ears-Puddles-Pools*;
The Gibbon-Climbs-The-Brittle-Tree;
The-Nunatak-Dissolves—Slowly;
the triptych many take to be
His-Father-In-A-Gunnysack,
Quite-Undisquieted-By-Death,
Descends-Into-The-Last-Crevasse;
Ten-Herdsmen-With-Ten-Staffs-Who-Track-
The-Ox-Within-The-Haversack;
The-Ox-Forgotten, Man-Remains;
Both-Man-And-Ox-Forgotten; *Ox-*
And-Man-Beside-Six-Hollyhocks;
The-Tousled-Ox-As-Patriarch;
Anarchic-Larch-And-Two-Bourgeois;
Nine-Nenuphars-And-One-Sitar;
His-Sister-Tends-The-Samovar-
His-Mother-Had-Forgotten; *Far-*
Beneath-Blue-Bluffs, The River-Roars,
'Your-Fate-Is-Thin, Your-Knowledge, Frayed';
The-Hungry-One-Descries-A-Plate
Of-Aubergines; *The-Oud-Awakes*;
Three-Winter-Winds; *The-State-of-Grace-*
As-Seen-Beyond-The-Eastern-Gate,
Though-Some-Say-None-Can-Emigrate;
and *Apprehensive-Men-Of-State,*
Who, Having-Drained-The-Earth's-Tisanes,
Replace-The-Fountain-Of-Chopin-
*With-Twenty-Stone-*Vespasiennes;
The-Exiled-Scion-Of-Sulmona,

Seated-On-A-Green-Veranda-
Overlooking-Green-Savannas,
Listens-To-A-Green-Charanga-
Flute; his scroll of *Brother-Sun-*
And-Sister-Water-Smile-Upon-
His-One-Grand-daughter-As-She-Walks-
An-Island-Shore; *Green-Reeds, Grey-Rocks*;
Two-Pastures-For-The-Tousled-Ox;
The-Sandarac-Of-Frau-Perforce;
Cascades-That-Cleanse-The-Heart-Of-Dust;
How-Many-Waves—as well as works
too numberless to be evoked
by rasp or sough—did he reject
rambunctious greens and rufous reds
and tans and zaffers and divest
his brush of all but white and black—
the only Least and Most we know—
in *Rabbits-And-Crows-In-The-Night-Snow*? »

3. The-Fourteen-Fundamental-Snows

«Or would Wen Tong—when he had gone
so far—have found he could forgo
still more, and shed The-Black-Of-Crows-
And-White-Of-Rabbits and devote
his brush to white and white alone,
in painting *Nothing-But-The-Snows*:

«Ungodly snows of Altyn Tag,
where the divine decline to slog—

no galligaskins of the gods
can find content in promenades
on summits folded, squeezed, compressed,
on ridges, spurs, compacted crests
like pyramids and cones, flat caps,
nodosities and blisters, blebs,
cusps, ledges, kéddahs, minarets,
humps, wens, and wedges, nesses, paps
(more shapes and shapelessness than we
have sins confessed *in pectore*)—
the renegade miscellanies,
deranged and derelict debris
of scarps so strewn with tangled scree,
collúvies and asymmetries—
as if the rind of Earth had meant
to mime the *mens* of man and smashed
the hankerings of Cosmoplasts
to edify a Mundus less
enthralled by rumpus, stour, and mess;

«and snows that overlooked the gods'
mistake in taking Ulu Dag
(that is to say, Olympos East—
if one is given to a Greek
gazetteer) to be Their-Peak,
their home, their haunt, their promenade
(until they heard that Hesiod
had trekked a statelier, more *echt*
Olympos farther west)—and yet,
since Deathless-Ones can never know
The-Very-End and, therefore, long

for *petite mort* with Mortal-Ones,
when gods return to Ulu Dag
with women snatched from valley floors'
astonished fields and arbors, or
when goddesses gambado with
the likes of an Anchises, it
may be the very snows that had
first overlooked the gods that then
attend their yens with white divans
whereon The-High delight The-Low
with eye and hand and thigh and slow
reflection, raptus, and caress
until The-Low at last forget
the death they bear when they beget,
and set aside the cry, 'Not Yet,'
that is to fill their final breath,
and murmur 'Now' and 'Here' instead—
at which The-Deathless can reflect
on radiance that intercepts
(much like the light the snows reject
that yet is given to reflect
and instantaneously bless)
only the intimates of death;

«bemusing snows of Helicon
that jar the telencephalon
until it is not sure if nine
or seven Nenuphars preside
over the dwellings of the mind
(and when they leave their mountain-side
and fountains, do they take the guise

of mothers, sisters, restless brides,
or blessed sedentary wives?);

«the vacant snows, where none abides
unless his squatter's rights provide
for swift eviction if he shows
the least reluctance to forgo
all solemn music from Compline
to Vespers—for In-Vacuo
(as ouds and shrewd sitars must know)
has need of Awe, but Con-Brio;

«susurrous snows of Hindu Kush,
where Stormont-Murphy Arctic Stoves
may serve to stave the clasp of cold
but cannot keep at bay the hushed
disclosure of The-Whitest-Wish-
That-Waits-In-Us, the itch of *Nichts;*

«volcanic snows that mask the ash
the cone of Etna resurrects
whenever it assumes that death
deserves new impetus and thus,
rehearsing *Furibundus*-Fuss,
deploys lapilli, magma, dust,
and, with a loud Pelean cloud,
removes the sanitary shroud
and frees the molten Lazarus
of our benighted Rum-Ram-Ruf;

«the snows of Ararat that feel

the force of an Ur-Father's keel,
the keel that salvages when *Nichts*
would render Will a derelict;

«the snows of Ida trembling still
when an Ur-Mother's fated cymbals,
caldrons, kettles, woks, and ladles
summon to The-Total-Table;

«gala snows that Marmolada,
Monte Mesma, Monte Grappa—
even far Thabantshoyana—
summon for their *gozzoviglia*,
festal fall of flakes, carousal,
buccal dance, romaika, revel,
winterwords and white arousal,
syllables and crystals—Wassail-
Of-The-Whitest-Particles;

«the drunken snows of Nysa that
still sleep in wine, the sleep of vats,
where Bacchus, born to Blanc de Blancs,
was swaddled in a soft snowbank,
though one who (after crossing sokes,
lagunas, pusztas, dongas, holts,
arroyos, wadis, wapentakes,
and sumps, and other quaking states)
had come to reconnoiter those
same scarps and slopes with soaked sabots
is often ready to intone—
The sleep of wine is sleep of hope,

in lees there lives Our-Second-Soul;

«the restless snows of ghauts and ghats,
of Ulugh Muztagh's crevices,
the yet-unmapped synaptic clefts
where Alexander-The-Sleepless
first taught his cilia to keep
their distance and denied to Sleep
dominion, lest his lamp be damped
and dreams defeat his vigilance;

«hermetic snows of Huascarán
that intimate The-All but let
their intimates divine the rest—
though no adepts have done so yet,
no herdsmen and no khidmutgars
who pace their tan and barren floors,
nor traffickers who can import
their prayer rugs from Kirsehir
or Karabagh and kneel therefore
in more accomodated fear
and, underneath that peak, implore;

«the snows of tedium, the Pure-
And-Ur-Ennui of blank couloirs
and khuds that bore: of Ahaggar,
of Lesser—and of Great—Khingan,
of Minor and of Gross Schreckhorn
(despite appearances, but one
same magnitude of tedium),
the snows inscribed with Why-Go-On?,

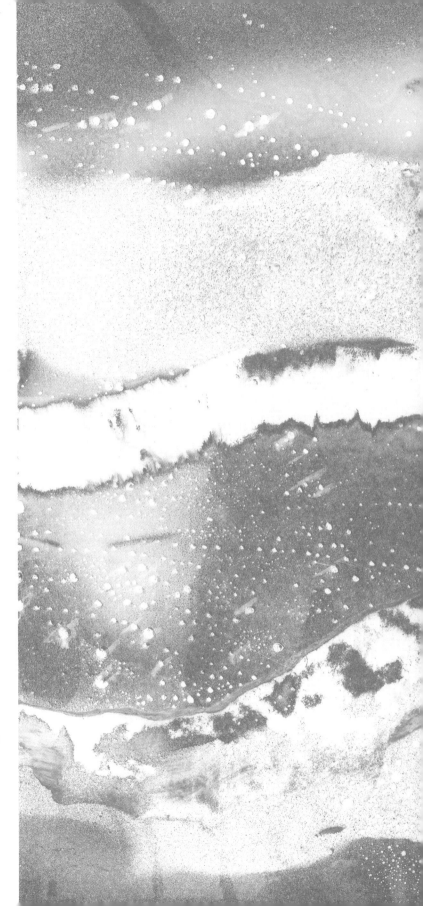

The Fourteen Fundamental Snows

But Are the Fourteen Neiges *Enough?*

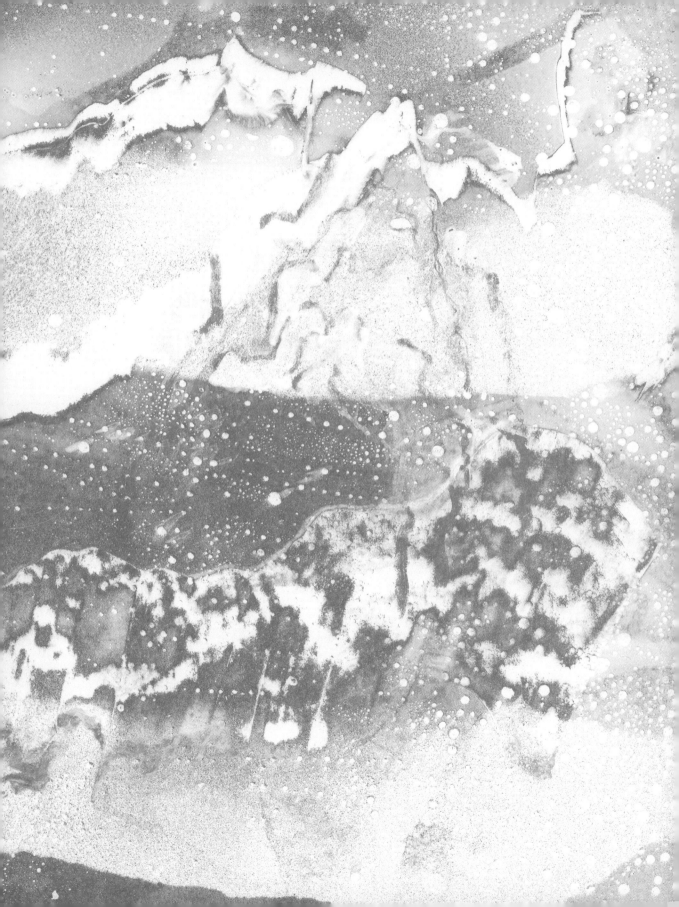

with What-Has-Been-Is-Yet-To-Come,
or—some allege—However-Cracked,
The-Same-Carafe-Serves-All-Who-Quaff;

«derisive snows of Gashberbrum,
The-Final-Frigidarium,
that summit where The-Flawless-Cause
must yield unto The-Padishah-
Of-Padishahs, The Awe-Of-Awes,
who strips the flagging Cogito—
already *sine ictu*, numb—
of both its blue surtout of *Sum*
and tan tarboosh of *Ergo*—though
a son of Karakorum, come
by way of Awe and then of Frau
Perforce, once he has thawed (and knows
that she is shelter, she will sew—
as soon as time allows—new clothes,
but now, beneath the lantern's glow,
upon his nakedness bestows
the warmth of her tisanes), avows
that he is far from certain how
divestiture had come about:
Was it the Cogito that lost
its *Sum*? Or *Sum*, its *Cogito*?
How hard it is to tally loss—
he says—when *Ergo* is forstraught
by any Awe-That-Is-Not-Mine-
Nor-An-Inhabitant-Of-Time,
allowing us no anodyne
or lenitive when soul would find

the innocence of an outcry
that does not mewl out 'Days-Awry'
or pule within the pit of 'I-
Have-Been-And-As-I-Am-Shall-Die'?»

4. But Are the Fourteen Neiges Enough?

«And would Wen Tong, if he had drawn
The-Fourteen-Fundamental-Snows,
have paused to let his lens repose
on whiteness other than the snows',
upon the candor of a breast
where one may take prolific rest,
the sweetest sabbath, some insist
(despite Ecclesiastesists,
who will, at most, consent to watch
but shudder at the thought of touch-
ing Any Thing that heaves or swells
as would the Grosse Fuge's viols),
or on the white of almond branch—
and, after his repose, have hummed
the softest of cesurasongs
and—*meno mosso, moderato*—
faithfully continued on
to other snows that drew his brush;
for fourteen *neiges* are not enough
when adepts have assured us eight
more snows still lie in white and wait
to congregate among The-Two-
And-Twenty-Snows (although a few

among The-Early-Elders-Who-
Had-Lived-Before-The-Giant-Thaw
enumerated eighteen more)
still visible from the moraine
of *mens* that overlooks terrains
as white as Adirondack nights
beneath the Ampersands' twin heights
or as the Engadine's firstlight,
that strikes the frets of snow and ice
and glacial waters with *Weissheit*;
and while a diptych thick with so
diverse a synagogue of snows
would have been like The-Manifold
or—some say—*Mannigfaltigkeit*
that whitened the December nights
of Königsberg when Kant was cold
(yet never loosed his fated hold—
no *Schnee* could lead his *Strasse* astray).
we know Wen Tong would never let
his brush relapse to care-lessness;
for though six months before his death
his dexter hand was rumored reft
and skewed by Dúpuytrén's disease,
his brush can well attest, his left
was deft enough were there the need
to paint with the precisest rage
and piety, *The-Final-Eight*:

«Eccentric snows of Tendai-san
beside the bridge of stone whose form
recalls a rainbow in the sun

(or sober Scrutinists insist,
a turtle's back)—together with
The-Tacit-Lioness who casts
(Ur-Mother-Of-The-Nought-And-*Nichts*)
her cubs down from the precipice
to see which of her sons resist—
and climb again to other tests—
and which fall prey to White-Abyss;

«assauging snows of Démaván,
that do not ask and not propound,
submitting to the valley sounds
of Disquisition's-Many-Gongs,
demanding nothing from the flow
of soughs and screaks and caterwauls,
of guile-and-bile-and-vaunt-and-gall's
geschrei, *fracásso*, flumps and yawls,
tracasserie and tíntamárres—
as if such clishmaclatter were
the sounds of a suitable sitar;

«the Guadarrama's snows that are
white emblems of departure for
the shepherd and for *buen amor*
the slopes of summer offered those
who cannot love among the snows
(but need spasmodic thraws and throes
when brambles, yarrow, grass are seen
beneath the bellished lens of green
that fears the White-Of-The-Unseen),
who with departure, never know

the winter gifts of Enthymeme—
when she has set aside her earrings;

«the tender snows of Puy-de-Dôme
that melt before they have become
a Dore, a Dogne, Garonne, a Var
and never can beget a Loire
(but Puy may be consoled by this,
if shared distress is demi-bliss:
the Sad-Seigneur-Of-Scrutinists—
Ovidius-The-Garrulous,
Sulmona's-Son, The-Banished-One—
despite devoted lens, neglects
and, when he would digress, forgets,
but, in his last *tristesse*, admits
that many transformations are
beyond the power of samovars'
tisaines, or tafia, pastis,
for these—and sober reveries—
may alter much, but not the This
when That is like tenacious schist;
deception waits in many shapes—
the Scrutinist consults with fears,
with *triste chair* and many tears);

«the early snows that, in descent,
rehearse the frost of early death—
October snows of Hoosac hills
when rufous leaves of maple fall
and fill the fishing-baskets far
beneath the bridge—a water wheel,

in the precocious ice, is still;

«the snows of nature—and the snows
of nurture, which bestows on those
who dwell upon descended snows
the igloo stratagems that, from
the matter they oppose, can form
The-Oval-Where-Our-Tale-Is-Told,
The-Dome-Wherein-The-Ebb-And-*Flux–
De-Bouche*, The-Sighed, The-Rasped, The-Soughed,
Become-Caress-And-Wound-And-Touch,
The-Effable, perhaps enough
to interpose, to interrupt
the silent soul when it beholds
The-Cold-That-Cannot-Be-Retold—
just as The-Great-*Cohoue*-Of-Clothes
(gamashes, spatterdashes, jupes,
galoches, galligaskins, hukes
and haiks and hems and sarks and snoods,
tight shintiyans and loose perukes,
wraprascals, togas, boas, daks,
yashmaks and yeleks, gunnysacks,
dalmatics, obis, our unpressed
paipaks and ponchos, petasos
and swaddling clouts and furbelows,
turncoats and tuckers, chudders, brogues
and pugarees and scuffed sabots,
surtouts and antigropelos
and prayer shawls) can interpose
between our bones and nature's snows—
or as, between The-Nunatak

and tendons, nerves, and ligaments,
there stands the warp of winterworks,
whale-fat and words and blood and breath,
as well as the adroit kayak's
fine Equilibria-That-Rack;

«and Snow-Of-Snows that—though beset
by thaws and throes—has made its home
along the metamorphic Mont
Parnasse—the vast and versal scarps
where hues of Alls and flecks of Parts
align, entwine, reside, abide
(or—when the dance is too defined—
collide) within The-White-Gavotte-
Of-*Neverending-Blanc-Des-Blancs*?»

5. *Since Even Snow of Snows May Thaw*

«Or was Wen Tong, who saw the flawed
divans of man from Tendai-san
to Phlegethon, more drawn to draw
(since even Snow-Of-Snows may thaw)
the dwelling place of his own face,
but seen as if inhabited
by *Alexander-The Sleepless*,
whose yesterday became today
so swiftly that he had no past,
no place that, though at hand, is yet
intact, inviolate, exempt
from memory's rapaciousness,

where one need not debauch, possess,
trespass or tamper or transgress
the boundaries of testament—
or by *A-Bearded-Hoarse-Savant,*
who had forgotten what his want
had wanted when the way it went
was past all paths that might have meant—
but then remembered Greta Lentz?

«Or, even as mimosa casts
still shadows on still waters when
the wind is indolent, was Wen
Tong more content with lines he limned
when idleness delivered him
to *Meeting-Places-We-May-Reach-
When-Neither-Scroll-Nor-Brushes-Seek?*»

6. *To Stand in Silent Synagogue*

But while persistent Paraphrasts
are unappeased until their Nine
Interrogations have again,
again been asked (as if a sign
without a gloss were like a Seine
without its banks, or like a man
bereft of black surtout and tan
tarboosh and vest when Boreas
and desolate Aporias
descend upon l'Impasse de L'Ouest
with their premonitory lance—

and every naked cul-de-sac
remembers that it will not lack
a last, intransigent divan),
The-Chastened and The-Patient and
The-Reconciled have only sought
to stand in silent synagogue,
to listen as Each-Query talks
(before its cadences are lost,
before the shade that opens on
the Promenade des Horizons
has been denied, forgotten, shut)
to them, to us, and to the heart
of Frau Perforce, and—though the dust
must overtake the prayer rugs,
precepts, divans, and palimpsests,
as well as those discarded drafts
inscribed when clement candles cast
their light upon the pinewood half-
moon table where he may have sat—
even to the *savantasse*.

NOTES

I met the *savantasse* through my son, Jonathan, who lived in Montparnasse, on the Rue Lebouis, from 1974 to 1978. The record of that encounter was substantially completed by 1978, but several portions were honed and supplemented in 1983 and then in 1985. For these refinements and additions, the testimony of Signora Enthymeme, Frau Perforce, and Angélique Abrí—though at times discordant—was most helpful. In the shadow of the Tower of Montparnasse, the Rue Lebouis and all the streets surrounding it have been totally transformed. Where change is so drastic and promises to be so irreversible, the reader charting this work's arrondissements may welcome a few notes. Angélique Abrí, in her *Scuffed-Sabots: Two-Guides-To-Parts-Of-Speech-Along-The-Rue-d'Assas*, does define the *savantasse* as a sciolist: one who makes a «vain show of superficial learning». And though the Rue d'Assas lies north of Montparnasse, she did pedal south; and her description is first-hand and somewhat accurate. And, in chanting of a sciolist, I may have been infected by my protagonist with smattering and approximation. But I have tried to keep these notes as unevasive as my own years and turbid memory allow. (Normally, page numbers are not needed for the following items; but where a poem is long and the reference point is small, page numbers are given.)

Firstlight

The «Piedmontese lakeside» is the eastern shore of the Lake of Orta at the point where the village of Orta San Giulio lies opposite the island of San Giulio. The zone is singularly prone to nocturnal storms; and after some seventeen summers there, I remember countless candlelights.

«Sulmona's central square» is the Piazza XX Settembre. There, since 1925, stands the statue of Ovid by Ettore Ferrari, a statue based on a sketch of the statue in Romania at Constantsa on the Black Sea, the sea that saw the exile and death of Sulmona's son.

Precautionary Prelude

A «*pinarium*» is a «*pièce où on fait l'amour*» (see the alphabetically ordered «Scoriae from *The Vast and Versal Lexicon*» at the end of my *Chelmaxioms*).

«*Moia biéda*» is the Russified spelling, not infrequent in the nineteenth century, of the Polish «*moja biéda*», «my sorrow», the words inscribed by Chopin on the envelope in which he placed Maria Wodzinska's letters to him. («*Moia*» is, too, visually closer to «*moira*» than «*moja*» is.) The chant of the «fountain of Chopin» may have been Op. 23, which the *savantasse* first heard as played by Soudaine Souplesse (see «The Ayre of And», pp. 130-31).

The «worn astragalus» of the *savantasse* may be the result of too many hazardous casts; as Frau Perforce often murmured, the Ephesians—and other Greeks—used the huckle-bones of animals for making dice. (To this, Maud Maraud would sometimes add: «And without Heraclitus' *coup de dés*, we would never have had Mallarmé's»).

Soudaine Souplesse once cautioned me that, though *agrypnia*, or sleeplessness, was shared by both the *savantasse* (pp. 18 and 127) and Alexander-The-Sleepless, the fact that the former was plagued by his *agrypnia*, whereas the latter longed for it («lest dreams defeat his vigilance», p. 177), should give me pause in weighing and reporting the words and humours of the *savantasse*; for his insomnia incited vagabond digressions, while that of Alexander encouraged resolute compression.

The three bill-board sentences contained in the «one-hundred-seventy-three majuscules» are unevenly divided between Mallarmé («The flesh is sad, alas, and I've read all the books», the first line of his «*Brise marine*» sonnet) and Pascal's *Pensées* («All the misery of man comes from one thing alone: his not knowing how to stay put in a room», Brunschvicg, 139; and «The eternal silence of these infinite spaces terrifies me», Brunschvicg, 206). For Enthymeme's variation on Mallarmé, see «The Ayre of the *Triste Chair*» (p. 32), and for her descant on the first of the Pascal graffiti, see «The Ayre of Albion» (pp. 58-61); for the *savantasse* and sundry Paraphrasts on the first of the Pascal graffiti, see «The Ode of the Scuffed Sabots» (pp. 76-78); and for an anonymous passerby on the second of the Pascal graffiti, see «The Ode of the Scuffed Sabots» (pp. 80-81).

The-Gazetteer-For-Sleepless-Gluteists is, clearly, often complemented by A. Dauzat and G. Deslandes' *Dictionnaire étymologique des noms de rivières et de montagnes en France*, with younger River-Hearers given to Ch. Rostaing's revised edition. And, despite the distance between Vaucluse and Montparnasse, cxlviii of Petrarch's *Rime*, with the twenty-three rivers in the first quatrain of that sonnet, may also have infiltrated the River-Hearers' reveries. As for the river Sambatyon, not to be found in either Dauzat-Deslandes or Petrarch, it rests its flow on the Sabbath, according to the rabbis consulted by Pliny the Elder (*Natural History* 31:34). But Josephus (*The Jewish War* 7:96-99) claims the opposite: for him the Sambatyon flows on the Sabbath and not on weekdays. For more on that river, see Angélique Abrí's *Scuffed Sabots*, where she arrays R. Akiva (*Sanhedrin* 65b), Nachmanides on Deut. 32:26, and many others.

For The-Tousled-Ox (p. 22 and then p. 25), both the *savantasse* and Schwarzseher had most in mind the *Ox and Herdsman* of Sekkayushi, the fifteenth-century painter (whose brush they had first met via another painting, his *Monju Bosatsu Dressed in a Robe of Braided Grass*, dated 1418, which they had found— somewhat north of Montparnasse—in the Musée Guimet). While in the *Ox and Herdsman* it is a «tousled herdsman» who «tends a large ox», epithets do migrate easily from a herdsman to his ox. Sekkayushi's painting probably illustrates one of the *Ten Oxherding Songs* (see Mikeyo Murase, *Japanese Art: Selections from the Mary and Jackson Burke Collection*, New York, 1975, pp. 103-05 and the references there, especially Jan Fontein and Money Hickman).

For the «Twelve-Pervasive-Passions» of Charles Fourier, see his *Le Nouveau Monde amoureux*; and for Wen Tong, see the following note—on «Before the Brush».

THE CRACKED CARAFE

Before the Brush.

The Ur-Wen Tong (or Wên T'ung), a native of Szechuan province, died in 1079. One repertory of signatures and seals carries for him the alias Yü-k'o, and Mr. Laughter and Mr. Stone Chamber as nicknames. The later Wen Tong, whose scrolls intrigued the Paraphrasts of Montparnasse (see «After the Brush», pp. 166-86), evidently had a more varied oeuvre than his earlier namesake. And his roaming seems to have included a fair number of versions of works by other painters, not least, Wen Cheng-ming and Shōhaku (see «Boatsongs», p. 40 and note, and «After the Brush», p. 182 and note). To the latter he *may* also be linked by the use of a predecessor's name rather than his own, for «most curious about Shōhaku's artistic lineage is his frequent signature using the name Soga Jasoku or Jasoku-ken . . . claiming himself [in the eighteenth century] to be the tenth-generation heir of the ink painter who lived in the fifteenth century» (Murase, p. 219). The Paraphrasts of Montparnasse, in their partial catalogue of the later Wen Tong, also include his versions of at least two of the *Ten Oxherding Songs—The-Ox-Forgotten, Man-Remains* and *Both-Man-And-Ox-Forgotten*—as well as a number of other ox-centered paintings. In none of these does the ox gore, though in at least one he runs the risk of being gored: *Pascal-Would-Gore-The-Patient-Ox*. (For the catalogue of Wen Tong's works, see specifically—among the pages of «After the Brush» already noted above—pp. 170-72.)

While Gallic botanists are able to provide details of the *hippocrépis* that repelled Schwarzseher but attracted his dog (see p. 75 and note—and, for more on the dog, pp. 117-19), it would seem to take a Paraphrast from South Carolina to enlighten one on the possumhaw of Wen Tong and whatever Sinic equivalent or kin that plant has.

The Ayre of the Triste Chair

Enthymeme may hum Bellini, but no one has ever found her to be a *somnambula*.

The cracked carafe of the *savantasse* did at times desert tafia, a molasses-based rum, for Australia's Baileys Bandarra Muscat, based on the Earthly Paradise, which Dante rightly locates in the antipodes (see p. 155).

Boatsongs

Though Wen Cheng-ming did paint two learned fishermen («indifferent to what is happening at the end of the pole»), his brushes never treated either the mountain of Tendai-San or its «extraordinary natural stone bridge», as did Soga Shōhaku. (For Wen Cheng-ming's fishermen, see Richard Edwards, *The Art of Wen Cheng-Ming, 1470-1559*, Ann Arbor, 1975, p. 128: and for Shōhaku, see Murase, p. 219.) But the later Wen Tong may well have fused the fishermen and the cliffs of Tendai-san: or—just as possibly—the *savantasse*, with the help of a cracked carafe, may have done so. For more on the bridge of Tendai-san, see p. 182 and note.

THE AYRES OF THE RESTLESS SÉDENTAIRE

An Ayre of Other Years

My first meeting with the *savantasse* had as its occasion typographic matters; I had wanted to see colophons of his own devising and samples of Giovanni Mardersteig's early work in Montagnola (on the outskirts of Lugano) before he moved to Verona. The knowledge and liberality of the *savantasse* was notable—and totally enlightening—whenever he touched on ems and ens. And my *Lied of Letterpress* of 1980, celebrating the craft of Barry Moser and Harold McGrath, not only received warm impetus from hours I had spent with the *savantasse* but took off from some of the lines I had allotted to this « Ayre of Other Years ».

The Ayre of Albion

Maud Maraud has pointed out that, though it is a sonnet that drew the *savantasse* across the Channel to Westminster Bridge, and another sonnet, Baudelaire's «*Les Chats*», that (together with Pascal) reinforced Enthymeme's defence of sedentaries (p. 59-64), even as still another sonnet, Mallarmé's «*Brise Marine*», provided Enthymeme with a point of departure for her response to the *savantasse* in «The Ayre of the *Triste Chair*» (p. 32), the only formal allusion to the sonnet is merely numerical: the use of fourteen members of one same rhyme family in consecutive lines (the last five lines of p. 58 and the first nine lines of p. 59). And of the eight lines in that sequence attributable to Enthymeme, Maraud would note that one line-end, «unallayed», lapses into assonance.

Enthymeme's details of what Kant did *not* do (pp. 62-64) betray little dependence on the memoirs of his life—published shortly after his death—by Borowski, Jachmann, and Wasianski. Frau Perforce, though of accord with the burden of Enthymeme's anti-peripatetic polemic, would have proceeded less obliquely in anything having to do with Kant.

Some mutter that I have mis-cited Frau Perforce in the penultimate stanza of Part Three: given her praise of «The-Near» and «our Here» (p. 66), she would never, even as concession, have allowed the *savantasse* to conjure feasting his eyes on the bakery windows of Poilâne (p. 68) when, close to home, on the Rue de l'Ouest in Montparnasse, he could have found the Société de Boulangers Israélites Réunis.

The Ode of the Scuffed Sabots

My compiling these notes in 1987, the *Millénaire des Capétiens*, does allow me to see that, even as early as 1983, some kind of Capetian frenzy must have been circulating among the Paraphrasts of Montparnasse responsible for pages 71-72.

For fuller details of the «*hippocrépis*» (p. 75), see Gaston Bonnier and George de Layens, *Nouvelle Flore—pour la détermination facile des plantes de la région parisienne*.

For Pascal as not only «*virginum ultor*» (p. 79) but «*aequitatis amator*», «*veritatis defensor*», see the epitaph for Pascal by A.P.D.C. (Aymon Proust de Chambourg).

For the anonymous passerby's cadenza (pp. 80-81) on the differences between Pascal and Leopardi (who «reclined behind a hedge / with nothing more than fifteen taut / hendecasyllables»), the seventh and eighth of those hendecasyllables of «*L'infinito*» do indeed bring Leopardi close to Pascal's fear, as the «man from Recanati» witnesses (or engenders?) «interminable spaces . . . and more-than-human silences»; but Leopardi finds in that proximity to fear a path through and beyond it to his final lines: «Thus my thought drowns in this immensity, / and it is sweet to shipwreck in this sea». But Frau Perforce has pointed out to me that the «interminable spaces» of Leopardi, though initially speechless, are overarched by way of the *voice* of the wind and the «*sound* of the present» age. Yet Pascal, on his side of the hedge, is after all fully entitled to stop at «speechless space», to shun the shipwreck simile, and to find in the motley sounds of tramontanas and mistrals, not human speech but sounds «that cannot answer any plea». Giuseppe Ungaretti was probably the first to juxtapose *L'infinito* and Pascal's *Pensées*, 206; the passerby may well have been somewhat indebted to him.

Four Phantoms from the Far Savanna

Frau Perforce, who had heard from the *savantasse* the same four dreams that he murmured to me, noted that a «Targuman» (p. 83 and then p. 85) is, in Old Arabic, an «interpreter», just as, in Aramaic, a «targum» is a «translation, interpretation».

For P. Kretschmer's etymological derivation of Penelope («whose doing is undoing», p. 83) from *péne*, «the warp of a fabric», and **elop*, cfr. ὁλόπτο 'to tear'», see Arie Hoekstra's note on *Odyssey* xiv, 162, in Vol. iv of the Fondazione Valla-Mondadori edition of the *Odyssey*, 1984.

THE MAIDEN NAME OF FRAU PERFORCE

Precepts of Frau Perforce

For Precepts xxix, li and, lxviii, Frau Perforce draws, respectively, on Descartes, Brecht and Plotinus. But when she cites Art. 135 of Descartes' *Les Passions de l'âme*, she abandons her normal exactitude and omits his careful explanation of *why* «the cause of sighs is different from that of tears». For, as Descartes sees it, while tears are prompted by the lungs being full of blood, it is almost empty lungs that prompt sighs when «some image of hope and joy opens the orifice of the venous artery» and «the little blood that remains in the lungs [after they have been drained by tears] suddenly falls into the left side of the heart»; and that artery stirs all the muscles of the diaphragm and chest, and air is «promptly pushed by the mouth into the lungs, to occupy the space that the blood has left behind; and that is what one calls sighing». But whether full or sparse in this precept, Perforce would surely expend no words and no esteem on Mallarmé's encomium of sighs in his ten-line «*Soupir*», which usually follows his «*Brise marine*».

Interrogations

«*Hyperdulia*» is the only instance I know where the *savantasse* used a technical theological term as vehicle for a metaphor (and he may well have learned the term from Maud Maraud). For Catholic theologians, *hyperdulia* stands between *dulia*, the level of service owed to saints and angels, and *latria*, the worship owed to God alone—with *hyperdulia* owed to Mary.

The «crepuscular fatigue» of Frau Perforce «that follows hard upon / an afternoon with Heidegger's / late lucubrations» did not proceed from the taxing joys of discovery but from the travail of drastic dissent as she read his *Vorträge und Aufsätze*. But that dissent extended, too, to his earlier *Kant und das Problem der Metaphysik*. Indeed, she cared little for current distinctions between the pre-*Kehre* and post-*Kehre* Heidegger, the man of Care or *Sorge*, and the man of passive waiting for unveilings; for her, after all, the «debate» (if that term is not too awry) between Cassirer and Heidegger at Davos in March of 1929 was already a debate between *claritas* and *crépuscule*. And she, for whom «woodways [or *Holzwege*] gave way to *vieux pavés*» when she «left the Black Forest behind» (Precepts VI and XXXVII), would have found warm reinforcement of her stance in Steven S. Schwarzschild's *Franz Rosenzweig and Martin Heidegger: The German and the Jewish Turns to Ethnicism*, a volume now in preparation.

The Symbolic Logician Curbs His Dog

The «kélev» (Hebrew «dog») of page 119 may be an infiltration from S.Y. Agnon's *Kelev Meshuga* («Mad Dog») novella into precincts more suited to Faust's poodle.

THE HALFWAY HOUSE

The Branch That Bears Two Ayres

«*Quid deus, unde nives*» (p. 147), not a question but a declarative in Ovid's introducing the teachings of Pythagoras (*Metamorphoses* XV, 69), becomes a question in the English that follows it here.

The Ayres of the Outworn

For more on the cliffs of Tendai-san, see p. 40 and p. 182 and their respective notes.

THE LIEDERBOOK OF SEVEN DEATHS

The Lied of Libation

In murmuring «Old usherette, I've come to see your black spectacle», *the savantasse*, greeting Frau Oublí, bends but does not snap Victor Hugo's salute to death.

THE WOMEN AT THE WINDOW-PANE

The Ayres of Angélique Abrí

For the bitterness («*amari aliquid*») of Lucretius' anatomy of love, digest the last two-hundred-fifty-one lines of Book IV of his *De rerum natura*.

AFTER THE BRUSH

If, in rendering the blustering of the Paraphrasts, I was able to call on their need «to chrónohótonthólogós» (p. 165), it is because the mother of Soudaine Souplesse was responsible for the French translation from English of Henry Carey's *Chronohotonthologos* (first acted in 1734) for the Carey Bicentenary revival of his play at the Théâtre de Galimatias on the Impasse de l'Ouest, in March of 1934. Angélique Abrí, in her *Scuffed Sabots*, took care to reproduce the yellowgrey handbills of both the 1734 and 1934 productions.

For the Paraphrasts' use of *Falak-al-Aflāk*» (p. 168), presumably the Islamic «heaven of heavens», Angélique Abrí's *Scuffed Sabots* records the Akkadian *pillaku* as forefather of the Biblical and Talmudic *pelech*, Targumanic Aramaic *pilcha*, and the Arabic *falaka*, originally «whorl, spindle», or «distaff», of which the later, derived meaning is «celestial sphere» (with *falak* in the singular and *aflāk* in the plural).

With urban renewal in Montparnasse, the sense of «*petite mort*» or «little death» (p. 174) as a locution for the peak of bodily delight seems to have fallen into disuse.

However distant Nysa is from Provence, the Blanc de Blancs to which Bacchus was born (p. 176) is probably the Otts' Clos Mireille, a blessing derived from shale soil together with the blend of sémillon and ugni blanc grapes.

If those Paraphrasts who include the «eccentric snows of Tendai-san» (p. 182) among the snows painted by Wen Tong are indeed correct, then his brush has given us a later version of Shōhaku's *Lions at the Bridge of Tendai-san*, where «a lioness hurls her newborn cubs off a promontory near the high stone bridge to test their endurance. She will care only for those cubs that manage to climb back to her by scaling the steep cliffs. . . . Some inevitably fail, falling thousands of feet to the churning waters below, while the lioness, a rather gaunt creature, watches . . . with an air of passive detachment». (See Murase, pp. 218-221, though the *savantasse* himself probably saw the «Stone Bridge by Shōhaku», *Kokka 118*, October 1899, p. 193.) For other possible links between Shōhaku and the later Wen Tong, see «Boatsongs» (p. 40) and note, and «The Ayres of the Outworn» (p. 128).

«*Neverending*» (p. 188) echoes the Italian «*neve*» for «snow» in light of the Paraphrasts finding, among *The-Fourteen-Fundamental-Snows* depicted by Wen Tong, the «gala snows» of Monte Grappa, Marmolada, and—not least—Monte Mesma, a slope above Orta San Giulio (for which village, return to the very first of these notes).

ACKNOWLEDGEMENTS

The early stages of my encounter with the *savantasse* were represented by the following poems that appeared in *Leaves of Absence* in 1976: «Four Fragments from the Far Savannah», the three parts of «Returning by Boat on a Cold River» (which was dedicated there to Bruce Bassoff, «savant of knots»), «Before the Brush», «Honey Soit Samba», «The Ayre of Angélique Abrí», the second and fourth of four «Apartsongs», «Legal Tender», and «Likeness». Those fourteen poems were often subject to revision in titles and text as this record of the *savantasse* became more imperative for me.

That process had its way-stations in the *Denver Quarterly* with revised versions of what had become «Four Phantoms from the Far Savannah» together with «The Ayre of the *Triste Chair*», the «Ayre of All», and, more recently, «Firstlight» and the first part of «The Ayre of Albion». The last four of these poems have not undergone any significant revision since then. In the interim, the «Ayre of Other Years», as indicated in my note above, had mushroomed into *A Lied of Letterpress* in 1980. But here it appears in its initial seed-state, sown by my meeting the *savantasse*. On the other hand, some earlier seed-states, in *Journeyman* (1967), grew strangely under the aegis of the *savantasse* and his friends : The «Symbolic Logician Curbs His Dog», which first appeared in *Furioso* and then in *Journeyman* with some eleven lines, once Schwarzseher was at hand, grew to sixty lines, in which form it first appeared in the *Pacific Review*; the untitled first poem in the «Toward H. Daimonios» sequence had two of its lines grow into «The Lied of Frau Oublí», and «From Patagonia» found its final form as the third of the «Ayres of Angélique Abrí». The fourth section of «After the Brush»—«*But Are the Fourteen* Neiges Enough?*»—first appeared in a New Directions anthology of the ten American and ten Italian poets whose work was dealt with in Poetry-Genoa-New York in 1980.

For his careful assembling of *Oxherding* material, despite the pressing demands of his own volume on the relations between Manet and Mallarmé, I am indeed grateful to Harry Rand. He gave me much that the *savantasse* himself was too distracted to provide, even as Riccardo Contini helped me when I mislaid my copy of Angélique Abrí's *Scuffed Sabots*.

Robert Richardson, Thoreau's biographer and transcriber of the Romauntsch epigraph on the facade of a house at La Punt in the Engadine («*In liberted e proporziun / prosperescha / creaziun*»), patiently followed—and urged on—the many stages of these annals of the *savantasse*: may he forgive a protagonist not always given to *proporziun*. And Richardson, Vittore Branca, Steven Zwicker, Paul Mariani, and Seymour Mandelbaum, through the example of their work, have abetted my sense of the historian's, biographer's, and poet's recollections as often thick and tangled, partisan, polemical, approximate—and vital. And sometimes even ecumenical.

In charting the shared course of type, text, and image, Barry Moser was the magisterial artifex of five volumes. Time, place, and affinity have now brought me close to the art of Marialuisa de Romans: her *Ovidiane* sequence of paintings complemented *Ovid in Sicily*, just as her Homer drawings will complement my forthcoming translation of the *Odyssey*; and her drawings for this *Savantasse* volume are the first stations of her *Savantasse Scrolls* sequence of paintings. Throughout that course with Moser and de Romans, Czeslaw Jan Grycz has been a constant helmsman.

The presence of my son, Jonathan—like that of Daniel Feldman and Walter Stiller—has been indispensable on occasions as countless as candlelights in Orta San Giulio.

The text of this Convivio Book, designed by Libero Casagrande and Czeslaw Jan Grycz, and published by Sheep Meadow Press in collaboration with the Euryalus Foundation of Siracusa and New York, was composed in an adapted version of Scangraphic's Monotype Bembo by the Istituto Grafico Casagrande of Bellinzona in Ticino. Pieraldo Vola then printed the text and color-plates at the I.G.E.R. in Rome. The endpapers' emblem was adapted by Marialuisa de Romans from a cul-de-lampe by the later Wen Tong that appeared in the second edition of Angélique Abrí's *Scuffed Sabots.* This volume was printed in November of 1987.